EDDIE
PETER C. CROPSEY

ISBN: 1500989142
ISBN 13: 9781500989149
Library of Congress Control Number: 2014915838
CreateSpace Independent Publishing Platform
North Charleston, South Carolina

Put off concerning your former conduct, the old man which grows corrupt according to the deceitful lusts, and be renewed in the spirit of your mind, and that you put on the new man which was created according to God, in true righteousness and holiness.

—The Apostle Paul
Ephesians, 4:22–23

When you get up in the morning two guys are gettin' up with you: the old man and the new man. You're gonna sit down with both of 'em at the breakfast table. What you gotta do is take the oatmeal away from the old man and pass it to the new man, giving him a double portion 'cuz the guy that eats good is gonna be the guy with the strength to win the day. In fact, then just take the old man out back and bust a cap in his head and then go in and pray with the new man.

—Eddie Wilkins

CHAPTER 1

As you may remember from the last time we were together I had left the club run, which was at a lake about thirty miles east of Modesto, California, supremely stoned on mescaline, heroin, and meth, not to mention at least a half-pint of Jim Beam. It was a beautiful summer morning, and I was flying down that gently curving country road. I was rippin' along at about sixty when a subtle noise coming from my open belt drive insisted on my attention. Normally a quick glance would have been all I dared risk at that speed, and knowing my bike better than I knew, well, anything, it should have been all that was required.

But to my dismay, when I looked down I discovered there was a dachshund-sized dragon flying along next to my bike breathing flames and smoke. It was common for me to see things like that in the late sixties and even the early seventies but this was nineteen hundred and eighty-one, so it distracted me, particularly when it looked up and announced:

"You are about to eat it bad, boy!"

Yeah, I got distracted, and when I looked up it was just in time to see my front wheel leaving the edge of a twenty-foot embankment. And eat it bad I did...

The only one to see my wreck was an old farmer whose field I landed in, and he pulled me in out of that field. His name was Joseph Miller. From the moment I first laid eyes on Joseph Miller the simple presence of the man brought me face-to-face with the truth. I was nothing but a punk in a tattoo suit. I was a waste of space and air armed with a pistol, a grip of bad habits, and a broken decision maker.

This man represented everything good and true, represented everything a man should represent: a love for God and country, an unflagging loyalty to his family, and the values that it takes to raise that family. He had carved out a life for himself in this world by the sweat of his brow and the integrity of his heart. His hands were busy hands, workman's hands, rough and strong hands as rough and strong as the man himself. Being around him clearly illustrated how far off the beam my life had gone. And yet in spite of my tattoos, my dirty boots and 501s, my whiskey-sour stench, and my saucer-sized pupils he was disposed kindly toward me.

It seemed as if he saw me for what I could have been and not what I was. He had raised two strong sons—perhaps it was in his mind that if I had been his son I could have been like Bo and Billy, I would have had some direction, some guidance. I might have been solid and right, not broken and addicted. I know that as I lay there on the big leather couch and looked around the living room of his old farmhouse—a house that was made by his hands and showed love and attention in every beam and stone—and at the beautifully framed photographs that chronicled the life of his family, it surely crossed my mind:

What if I had been this man's son instead of the son of a pot-smoking, hippie nudist who really had no interest in being a father?

I had been on his couch and under his care for the last twenty-four hours. Joseph's wife, Joanne, had died of cancer in their home five years before and Joseph had given me three bottles of her leftover pain meds. Even years after the expiration dates they still packed a wallop and it was under their ministrations that I had taken a soul-searching trip through the past.

This salt of the earth, self-made man who had carved out a life for his family on this 120-acre farm, and who had shown me a kindness when he didn't have to, well, he had caused me to think about the self-centered, debauched life I was living. I mean, how did I become this heroin-addicted, prison-bound fool riding full speed ahead on a hell-bound train? Lying there on his couch and riding that wave of opiated semiconsciousness, I took a trip back to the beginning of it all. I took a trip back through the file cabinet of painful memories and bad decisions, I revisited the people and places that had shaped me, and after all was said and done I came to the realization that I was one seriously broken individual. Not just the broken from the accident—a marrow-deep, soul kind of broken.

I had remembered one recurring vision I had had all my life, but that hadn't visited me in so long I had almost forgotten it. It was the vision of a man hanging bloodied on a cross and He would look up and say to me:

"I love you, my child, and I will always be with you."

I hadn't seen that man for a very long time and I wondered if I had just gone too far, or if He became tired of my seemingly endless cascade of poor decisions and selfish actions.

I was marinating in all this stuff when I saw the Ranchero trailing a plume of summer dust, making its way down the long dirt road that led from the highway to Joseph's farmhouse.

As we pulled away from the farm I could feel the anxiety coming off of Stormy as powerfully as you can feel the angst when you're standing right in front of the PA column at a punk show. She was gripping the steering wheel of the Ranchero so hard her knuckles were white and she was chewing her bottom lip vigorously. This was totally out of character for Storm, who was usually in complete control of her emotions.

"I'm strung out, Eddie."

I had to think about that revelation for a minute before I answered. I had known, of course; all the signs had been there plain to see. The next-door neighbor Jack was a lightweight dealer, and I had seen Storm slipping out to go over to his place a couple of times. When she returned she was different in a way only another junkie can know. Storm's husband Ricky had been killed on his Panhead by a drunk lady and left Storm behind with two little girls, Margie and Ruthie. The grief she lived in had found its relief in the heroin that came from helpful neighbor Jack.

"Yeah, I thought so, and you know I'm gonna beat Jack blind, don'tcha?"

"Eddie, you are not in any condition to beat anybody in any way. And besides, Jack is no longer the problem."

In the wreck I had gained a broken wrist, a broken collarbone, and a few broken ribs, so Storm was right—it was gonna be a couple of days before I was in any kind of shape for beatin' on Jack.

"Then what is the problem, sis?"

The dams that were her bottom eyelids gave way and rivers began to pour from her eyes. I knew this was the beginning of that bone-deep soul weeping that overcomes every fiber of your being.

"Pull over."

She did, and when she had stopped she slumped over on me and it began. The pain of her weight on my wreck-injured frame was monumental, but it was nothing compared to the pain I felt in her shrunken little body. I hadn't really noticed how skinny she had gotten since Ricky was killed. Her tiny frame was racked with spasms of emotional agony and I realized that I hadn't seen her cry since the accident. She had been stoic at the funeral, her face set and filled with the resolve that she was going to mother the girls and weather the storm. At first she only used the chiva to get through the darkest moments of that storm, but the spirit of heroin is a cunning demon and he whispers sweetly in your ear from the very first shot:

"C'mon, you know you want me right now. I'll make everything all right. I promise."

She desperately needed everything to be all right and so she gave in to his solicitations. Now he had her in his viselike grip. All of the pain she had been denying, stuffing way down deep inside of herself and burying with syringes full of deception came vomiting up out of her and she just wept into me, her little back heaving as she was racked with sobs. I just held her and waited. After quite a while she shifted her weight so she could look up at me. She must have seen me wince. She sat up suddenly.

"Oh, I'm so sorry, Eddie. Are you okay?"

"I'm fine, girl. Can you talk to me? What's going on?

"Two guys have been staying at Jack's and they have taken over his house."

"Who are they?"

"I think they just got out of Folsom. One guy is really big and his name is Billy. The other guy is a lot smaller but is way more scary and his name is Chris. He has death in his eyes, Eddie."

She began crying again, big giant tears. I could almost see my face reflected in them they were that big.

"He came to the door and introduced himself but it felt like a threat. He was really staring at the girls like he was weighing the liability of them being there. I'm scared of him, Eddie. It's like he's casing my house for some kind of evil thing."

I knew who they were. Billy Wills was a born-and-raised Sacramento boy. From what I knew he came from a good family who lived in Orangevale. He had been raised right, played all-star football in high school, and then one day he did a shot of dope. He was smart and he had breeding, but that didn't keep the cops from busting him for assault and robbery when he was eighteen. Now at almost thirty years old he had earned a reputation in the prison system and on the street, although he was rarely out for more than a minute.

Chris Dalton was a completely different story. He was raised in Modesto by seriously alcoholic parents who communicated by beating each other with whatever was close at hand. Chris got more than his share of the beatings and by the time he was twelve he was in reform school. He was made a ward of the state at fourteen and grew up in youth institutions until he was old enough for prison. He was mean, cunning, and smart.

"Stormy, turn the car around. We gotta go get Blue."

It was about noon, more than twenty-four hours since I rode my bike off that twenty-foot embankment. The old farmer Joseph Miller had seen me flying through the air but no one else had. He hooked a flatbed trailer up to the tractor he had been disking his alfalfa field with and came and hauled my broken body to his farmhouse. My bike was left where it lay and I wasn't concerned. No one could get to it without going right by the house. Joseph and Storm had loaded my twisted scooter on the trailer Blue and I towed up from the OC.

We must have been a curious sight as we slowly made our way down the dirt road to the lake where the club run was in progress. I say this because a little crowd was forming around the twelve-gauge-toting prospect at the entrance. Down into camp we went, a hot-rod Ranchero with a beat-and-bandaged guy riding shotgun, a chick driving, and a twisted and broken Harley trailering behind. It took a moment for the boys to recognize me with the turban of bandages on my head and the makeshift sling on my shoulder, but when they did it caused a ruckus.

Monkey Man and Danny Mac charged the truck and were practically in the window before Storm could even get stopped.

"Oh man, what happened, bro? Look at you, and oh no! Man yer bike…It's…it's bad!"

With bikers there was always more concern for the condition of the bike than the person. People heal on their own or die; bikes have to be remade. That takes time and money, both of which are often in short supply in the life.

"I never shoulda let you gobble that tablespoon of Cocoa, man. I knew it."

Monkey Man was the purveyor of a substance we called Nestlé's or Cocoa and it was Nestlé's Quik mixed with lots of mescaline. We could have called it Quick, except then it might have been confused with the meth that, along with Kessler's blended whiskey, was the staple diet of the club. I had eaten a good tablespoon of that chocolate mescaline before I left yesterday.

"No, man, it's all on me. Hey, Monk, we've got an emergency in Sac-town. Where's Blue?"

" I dunno, man. Prospect, go find Blue right now and do it runnin'. Hey, Stormy, it's good to see you. I was really sorry to hear about Ricky; he was a righteous dude. If you ever need anything you know who to call, right?"

"Yeah, I know Monkey. Thanks a lot."

The boys were a little uncomfortable with Stormy's grief so after a minute or two of boot shuffling in the dirt they just kind of sauntered off, mumbling their good-byes. My mind was already working overtime at the news of these latest developments at the place Blue and I had been head-quartered since we left the OC a few months ago.

Billy and Chris both making parole at the same time was not fortuitous for us. Sacramento was kind of on loan to us because when we had shown up all the serious white boys were locked up, leaving the town wide open. Preda-tors are very territorial over the areas inhabited by their prey. To guys like me and Blue, or Billy and Chris, the prey were always the bottom-feeders—the addicts and two-bit hustlers that didn't have the heart for prison and there-fore wouldn't take the kind of chances that yielded the big paydays.

For guys who lived a large part of our lives in prison these lesser crea-tures provided a myriad of services. They moved out of their bedrooms and onto the couch when we showed up at the door. They ran errands that were too troublesome for us. They provided intel on who was up to what on the streets. And they forfeited whatever they had to shoot, eat, drink, or drive until we could make that big hit and get into a nice hotel.

Sometimes the cuffs would go on again before the big hit came and all we were left with was the satisfaction of knowing that we had had our way with the neighborhood and our ability to terrorize the poor, white-trash ghetto was alive and well. We were, after all, the undisputed kings of the trailer parks and the low-rent apartment projects. Once we were again tucked neatly in our six-by-nine cells the bottom-feeders would get to pa-rade like roosters saying:

"Yeah, the boys were stayin' at my pad this time until they got gaf-fled up again."

I realize I sound a bit condescending and so let me clarify. I have taken that fall from champ to chump, left alone on the street, the last one not busted. Without Blue my game would quickly slip away and I would find myself living in garages or some stolen, broken-down camper on the side of some house, barely hustling enough dope to stay well, and drinking cheap screw-cap wine when the cottons were too dried out to beat again. Oh yes indeed, I was a gangsta…Alas, I digress…

The look on Blue's face as he came running up from the lakeshore was one I had rarely seen. He looked incredulous. His eyes were wide open as was his mouth, and I could tell that the sight of my twisted bike on the back of the Ranchero and me all bandaged up in the shotgun seat had shocked him badly. But the news I was about to deliver would land the final blow in this sudden sobering up process.

"What happened to you, Eddie? Oh man, yer bike is toast!"

Always the bike…

Something about Blue never failed to put me at ease and make me feel comfortable, so I replied:

"Who goes swimmin' with their boots on except someone who is scared of little squishy crawly things getting between their toes?"

Blue was stripped to the waist and lake water was collecting in a puddle at his feet around his well-worn Chippewas. Droplets glistened in his hair and his beard and dripped down across his bare chest. The deep concern he had for me was etched into his features.

Suddenly everything became very still and my awareness of the summer sun, the gentle breeze rustling the leaves of the gnarled old oaks in this meadow, the melody of the birds' songs intensified. I became acutely aware of Blue and Storm; I could almost feel their heartbeats. I was overcome with a deep love for these two friends.

Now Blue was leaning in the window of the Ranchero and Storm was leaning over me toward Blue. I was right in the middle, with both of them just inches away and the moment manifested itself to all of us. It was a monumental moment. It was a sense of family and belonging so intense it was tribal. It was a very brief glimpse into purity and perfection that those of us living in the life rarely if ever get to feel. Nothing was said but everything was communicated.

"Yeah, my feet are sensitive," Blue said. "So what?"

Storm had shown up full of anxiety, but now she knew that everything would be fine; I knew it too. Like I said, something about Blue put me at ease, made me comfortable. There was a synergy with us—we were more together than we were apart. So much more…

Blue had a girl named Crissy once. Relationships get twisted up and convoluted when everybody is living on speed and heroin so she split one day. About a month later she called from a little town north of San Francisco. She said she wanted to come home but she had hooked up with some dude in a motorcycle club and he wouldn't let her leave. Blue asked her:

"What motorcycle club?"

She replied:

"The Puddle Butts."

I'm kidding, but who cares about the name? It was just some small club in a small town, trying to be outlaws. Blue asked me:

"You ready for a little ride?"

"Naturally."

We put pistols and ball-peen hammers in our bedrolls, filled a dozen syringes with heroin and speed and put them in the little black case (*you remember the little black case from* Dead Man Waking, *right?*), slipped a couple of pints of Kessler's in each of our vests, gassed up, did a shot, and hit the road. We left the OC at about ten in the morning and rode 90 miles an hour all day.

Stopping only to gas up, take a leak, and do a shot, the pints we passed back and forth at freeway speed, we pulled into that little town about midnight. Crissy had given Blue directions to the clubhouse and we were about a block away when we stopped to transfer the ball-peens and pistols to our waistbands and we just rode on in.

The prospect at the front door got a hammer to the breastbone for his attempt to deny us entry; surprisingly, he was the only security they had. Like I said, small town, small club, overconfident in the false belief that they were the biggest fish in the pond.

Identifying the president was easy. There were only three patch holders besides him in the clubhouse and he was the one with the puffed-up chest. As quick as a water moccasin slippin' through a bayou swamp Blue had his pistol rammed into the side of this cat's head.

"If things go south here you have only yourself to blame, 'cuz I just came for one thing. Where is Crissy?"

"I can have her here in ten minutes."

"You do that, and make sure she has her gear with her, 'cuz she'll be leavin' with us."

Blue and I were back to back. I could feel his commitment to this course of action right through his leathers. Man, he was always a cool character! He had his pistol all up in that dude's grill and I had mine trained on the rest of the room. There wasn't gonna be any fight here. They didn't know who we were or who might be with us, they only knew that this had gone down fast, and the dark quick energy we brought to the room was something they were unfamiliar with. It was the real deal. Something they thought they had but seriously didn't.

"Hey, man, we're cool, just take her and split."

The prospect with the caved-in chest kind of crawled in the door and Blue told him:

"Prospect, get up and put everybody's guns, knives, or whatever on the table here."

That yielded a couple of Buck folders, a bowie, and that was it, nary a pistol in the place. The "P" made a phone call and after about ten minutes of these guys all starin' at the floor a bike pulled into the driveway. Crissy came flyin' through the door and jumped into Blue's arms.

"You came, you came!"

Trailing along behind Crissy came a somewhat dejected but resigned-looking young biker who I recognized immediately as having salt. I didn't figure Crissy would be with some poop butt, but this guy carried himself like upper crust. He was young but I could see him callin' the shots up here one day. He walked right up to Blue and put his hand out.

"Rowdy Ralph."

"Blue."

"Sorry, man."

"It ain't on you, Young Blood."

We live in a different world, a very different world indeed.

As we were preparing to say our sad farewells and Blue was strapping Crissy's bag to his bike I heard him say to her:

"Good-looking kid. You sure you wanna split?"

"At least he doesn't have a needle in his arm before his feet hit the floor in the morning."

"Like I asked, you sure?"

"Yeah, yer my man, Blue, for better or for worse."

Three months later Crissy was dead from an overdose.

We checked into a motel down the road and headed back south on a bright clear morning. So that's how it was for me and Blue. When we were together we had the juice card in a very big way. We just had a thing, a synergy, we knew there was nothing we couldn't do and no place we couldn't go.

CHAPTER 2

Storm told Blue the same things she had told me as Blue was packing up. In about ten minutes we had his gear all stowed in the back of the Ranchero and he was following us up the road, headed toward an encounter with a couple of men who were cut from the same cloth as us. I was sure that it would all work itself out once we were all face-to-face. I was equally sure that North Sac was too small for all four of us to be runnin' our drag so I thought we'd probably head back to the OC. One thing was for sure: before we left I was gonna get some of Jack on my boots. That was a given. Jackboots, that's funny…

I positioned the rearview mirror in such a way that I could rest my head on the headrest and watch Blue ride. Storm had a Bob Seger cassette in the deck and it sounded good:

"Beautiful Loser, where you gonna fall?"

Where was I gonna fall? Had I just fallen? My body and my bike were both broken and surely to most it would look like I had fallen. But it didn't feel like I had fallen, maybe just turned a page. It seemed that no matter what happened to me or whatever I did to myself I was never cognizant of the danger I was in. I always just seemed to see events as doors leading to more and different doors.

If I got arrested, well I knew how to do time, just cut everything loose, stand strong and make the best of it. If I got ripped off, I didn't get all emotionally distraught over it, I just retaliated at DEFCON level 1 and moved on. No big deal…The fact that my life was a million miles south of normal, or good, or healthy, or wholesome, or even going anywhere, but instead was in fact plummeting toward the grave, well, it just escaped me completely. The truth is that my life had been one long fall—I was always falling and yet never reaching the bottom of that fall. At least not so far.

I realized I hadn't done a shot since before the accident. Out of gratitude and respect I wasn't going to shoot dope in Joseph's house even though

I had several outfits prepared and ready to go in my saddlebags. Joanne's pain meds had kept me well—better than well, actually—but now that we were under way my mind kept gravitating to the leather bags lying at my feet.

"Beautiful Loser, read it on the wall, and realize you just can't have it all."

I knew the Demerol and morphine combo was wearing off when I leaned up to try to position myself so that I could grab those bags. Man, I hurt in a major way. I was thinking it might be time to put pretense to rest as far as Storm was concerned. I wrangled those bags up on the bench seat between us and managed to get out the bandana that held the dope. I had left the case with Blue and so I had four syringes just wrapped in a rag. It was OC orange at that.

"Storm, gimme yer arm."

She looked at me in a quizzical way that asked, *Really Eddie, are we going there right now?*

I wrapped that OC orange bandana around her bicep, slapped the vein at the crook of her elbow to bring it up, and I slipped that rig right in. Direct hit—man, I was good! I guess I must have been kind of mad at her for getting strung out with two kids to care for because as soon as I saw the blood register in the rig I just slammed that plunger home. The Ranchero was almost in the ditch before I reached over and grabbed the wheel.

"Whoa, Eddie, what the heck was that?"

She was holding her chest and her eyes were as big as dinner plates. And then just as quick as she had rocketed up into the stratosphere I watched all of that electric shock leave her and I watched her eyes go pinned as the heroin overpowered the speed. She just kind of melted. She had a little trouble keeping the Ranchero between the lines for a minute as the two drugs in her fought for dominance but after a while they began to blend and she got a hold of herself. What in the world made me do stuff like giving her a gorilla-sized speedball while she was driving? I was grinnin' like the Cheshire cat. When she looked over at me I could see that she thought I was crazy but all she said was:

"Man oh man, that was freakin' amazing!"

"Yeah, that's why people do it, right?"

That moment changed the landscape of my relationship with Storm forever and even now I wish I could undo what I did that day. That act of carelessness set in motion a series of events that would change all of our lives forever. I was bent on giving Jack an issue of serious pain and suffering for getting her strung out, but here I had just given Storm her first speedball. What kind of person was I? Well, I was still gonna beat Jack brain dead. He wanted more from her than just her food stamps and the Social Security check that the kids got from Ricky's death.

The part that haunts me the most is imagining the look on Ricky's face if he could have seen the life his two beautiful innocent daughters inherited on that day, in that moment. When I pushed that plunger in and that demonic concoction rushed into Stormy's bloodstream I had in essence given her the green light to just let it all go. I gave her permission to just *go postal*. You see, I had already decided to let it all go myself, and what is the old saying? *Misery loves company...*

That day the walls came down, any kind of reservations I might have had about this life were bulldozed down. I wasn't Joseph Miller's son, I was a son of the wind, I was a son of the dark, I was a lost boy.

I remember being eighteen and being sentenced to a year in the county jail for a residential burglary. I was one of the youngest guys in the felony tanks at the Orange County Central Jail. There were a couple of Chicano cats from the Barrio Delhi in there that I had met in Juvie and maintained relationships with. So I was feeling comfortable from the start. I was put in a four-man cell. Two of the three dudes already in there were in their thirties, both fighting armed robbery cases, and the third dude was Kyle Roberts. He was eighteen just like me. He had been charged with attempted murder for stabbing a homosexual who had picked him up hitchhiking and attempted to molest him. You all know I immediately had a kinship with Kyle.

We were on the second tier in H tank cell 3 and the cell next to us was an all-black cell. At that time they segregated the races by cell and not by tier or tank so you'd have a cell full of white guys, a cell full of Chicanos, and a cell full of black guys possibly all on the same tier. Orange County jail was mainly a white and Hispanic population, not too many blacks. Well, by the mouth on this one black guy in the cell next to us you would have thought that they were in the majority. I don't know why this knucklehead had singled out Kyle—maybe because he was young, maybe because he really didn't belong there and everyone could sense it, who knows? I do know that I got to hear it after count my first night there.

We were making coffee. One-pound bags of coffee were stolen from the chow hall, passed to an inmate with his tray in the chow line, and smuggled back to the tier. We would make "stufas," or "bombs," by wrapping most of a roll of toilet paper around the hand and then tucking the edges under. These would burn with a very hot, smokeless flame for quite a while.

We would put the grounds and water in a wax-coated paper milk carton. As long as there was water in the carton, even though it was paper it would not catch fire. After it boiled, a couple of drops of cold water dribbled across the top would cause all the grounds to go to the bottom and we could pour about a half a Styrofoam cup each for two people. In a four-man cell the "stufa" was always going. Every night, poker or spades and coffee till the wee hours.

"Hey young'un...You know yous gawan to the pentenchy, doncha? Ya'll know wassa gong happens to ya in dea. Ain't gonna be nawan to protecha up in dat beeg haaus!"

He kept it up for a while until finally his cellies told him to pipe down.

"So, Kyle, how long has this been going on?"

"Since that guy got here about five days ago."

"You know what he says is a real possibility, and the solution for what could happen up there lies in what you do right here. You gotta take a stand."

"I don't wanna cause any trouble that will mess up my case."

"That's a chance you might have to take. I'm just saying if you don't stand up to this guy now the word will get to Chino and it will follow you up North from there."

"Yeah, so what do I do?"

"Well, bro, I gotta make a name for myself too so, it's what do *we* do?"

"Okay, so what do *we* do?"

"When the doors open for chow we're gonna storm that cell, kamikaze style."

So sure enough, when they racked the doors for chow Kyle and I were poised and ready to rock and roll.

"Check it out, bro, it doesn't matter who you land on in there, jack the first dude in your path and don't let up, even when you hear keys jangling their way down the tier. It's gonna be over in forty seconds max, I guarantee it."

There were only three men in that cell and they were totally surprised when we rushed in. Kyle jumped on the one closest to the door. He was sitting on the bottom bunk tying his Converse All Stars. The one with the big mouth turned out to be a very light-skinned, redheaded fellow that would be called "high yaller" in some circles. I knew it was him because as soon as we came in he started getting loud.

"C'mon, white boy, I got sumfin fo ya!"

What he was really doing with all of this loud, false bravado was trying to attract the attention of the cops because he was nothing but a cell soldier and he was trying hard to get out on the tier and in the sight of the man. I was clobbering him, raining down combinations on his head as he made for the door.

Now to this day I don't know how this happened but somehow the inertia of our bodies—me pounding down on his head, him covering up and trying to push through me to get out—sent him flying out of that cell screaming. He went over the tier, fell the twelve feet to the first tier, and landed right on his head. His head split open like an overripe honey dew.

Everybody, the cops coming down the tier included, thought I threw him over. Bad for yaller but good for me and my rep. Kyle and I went to the hole for a week but when we came back we were established. Kyle got twelve on his case and I saw him often over the years, and he always thanked me for that day. It also definitely improved my position in the pecking order because the next time I got busted I got brand-new everything when I dressed in. Bonaroos, we called 'em. When my year was up and I actually served only nine months due to good time and work time, I went to stay at my mom's house.

CHAPTER 3

Jon Stewart and my mom had made it. They had become a successful architect/design team, big house in Newport, back and forth to Mexico all the time. It was actually my stepdad Jon who asked me to come and stay at the pad. He never said so but I knew he loved me. I was just like him, full of angst and fighting the world. A wounded animal backed into a corner, ready to lash out and bite at any hand, friend or foe. I had a 1954 Harley Panhead, one pair of jeans, one pair of boots, a couple of T-shirts, and a leather jacket. I had spent nine months doing burpees and push-ups, eating the carb-rich county food, and I was feeling pretty strong. I hadn't done a shot of dope since I got busted...well, a couple of times when an issue came my way inside, but not often.

I was on San Joaquin Hills Road on my way to my folks' house when sure enough, *whoop, whoop*, I got pulled over for *Ugly in Newport*, a serious offense there. I was getting the full roust from this cop and I was taking it like a gentleman.

"Yes sir, no sir."

A silver Mercedes pulled up behind the cop car and this athletic-looking fellow, dressed in tennis whites, gets out and says:

"Officer, is there a problem? This young man lives next door to me."

"Oh, Mr. Richards. No sir, no problem, we just don't get too many bikers around here so I was just checking him out."

"Well, I can vouch for him."

"That's good enough for me, then."

The cop pulled away and left us standing there looking at each other. I had no idea whatsoever who this cat was.

He stuck his hand out. "Rich Richards. We live next door to your folks."

"I'm Eddie. Hey, thanks a lot, that coulda taken all day.'"

"No problem. Say, my wife and I, her name is Candy, we have a Bible Study at our house tonight. There are a few young people who come. Why don't you check it out."

There it was. The Man, the cross, my knees go weak, and I begin to tremble. That word, "Bible," it calls to some very deep place in me. I see Him:

"I love you, my child, and I will always be with you."

"Uh, what time, sir?"

"It's Rich, and we start at seven. But if you come at six thirty you can eat and meet some of the young guys."

"You know what? I'll be there. Oh, how did you do that—with the cop, I mean?"

"My father-in-law is on the city council and is a big supporter of the police department."

Big Canyon is a gated community and so I rode around the gate and gave the guard a one-finger salute. I got about a block in and turned around. I went to the guardhouse, threw down my side stand, and walked up to the guard, my hands spread and open in front of me.

"Man I'm sorry, I'm a jerk. My folks live at 12 Burning Tree, I'm staying there for a while. My name is Eddie."

"I like yer Panhead."

I was flabbergasted.

"Uh, thanks. It's a '54."

"My name is Joe. You just keep ridin' around the gate if I'm workin' and make a little noise for me, but shut it down after a block or so, so the folks don't get to complainin'."

I put my hand out and he shook it, good and firm, like he meant it. Maybe I could do this. Maybe I could fit in this world somewhere. I began to look forward to the Richards' Bible Study. I began to have some hope. I was clean, I was strong—yeah, I was, wasn't I?

I rang the bell on the Richards' massive front door at about six thirty-five. There were already a few vehicles in front of the house. They all had the telltale earmarks of surf vehicles. The two boards on the racks atop the Toyota pickup were a dead giveaway. The door swung open abruptly and I was face-to-face with this huge smile framed by a mane of shoulder-length, curly blond hair.

"Hey, praise the Lord, bro! I'm Craig, you must be Eddie!"

He was working my hand like it was a pump handle on a well and he was a thirsty ranch hand.

He abandoned that after a minute and switched to the bear hug. I smelled patchouli and sea salt. God had always been tracking me. He found me again that night and it was cathartic, revolutionary, astounding, and miraculous.

I was introduced to the crew: Craig, his girlfriend Leslie, Ernie, Rod and Gary (brothers), Rich's wife Candy, and a few other folks, but those were the main players in my experience. We noshed on cheese, hard salami, and crackers, and drank Cokes. Candy donned oven mitts and pulled a giant shepherd's pie from the oven. Everyone there was extremely beautiful—I mean, they were all physically handsome but there was something else going on. There was a shine about them and it was very magnetic. The talk, the laughter, it all had an ethereal quality to it. I remember thinking later on as I lay in bed:

Could they all have been angels?

The Richards' kitchen was huge, the whole house was huge, but in the kitchen there was a big rectangular oak table with about twelve chairs around it. When we all had sat down to eat every chair was filled and I thought:

Like the Last Supper.

Rich asked Craig to pray for the food and that is when it all began. I had never heard anything like it, or rather I had never felt anything like it. It wasn't a long prayer, he just said:

"Oh Lord, we are so grateful for You, for Your provision. Thank You, Father, for calling us to Yourself. Please bless this food and this time we are together. Oh, and Lord, thank You for bringing Eddie. In Jesus's name we pray, amen."

The words were simple but the heart that brought that prayer to Craig's lips was what utterly broke me down. I looked around the table at all of the faces there and each and every one held a peace and a totality I had never seen before. When I say a totality, what I mean is that not one person who was there was not completely there. They were very, very present. In a group of a dozen people there is always going to be at least one person who is thinking of somewhere else, some other person, place, or thing that will be vying for his attention. With a group of folks there will normally be some sense of distraction, however subtle, that succeeds in creating a sort of separateness.

With those folks, at that table there was an intense unity. I had read something in the Bible once and it came to me:

"Body of Christ."

Only a week before I had been in a sea of men and noise—a cold, concrete and steel box of woe. From early morning until late at night there was no quiet and the conversations and the yelling, all were heavily punctuated with profanity and the expressions of the thinking of vulgar and uneducated minds. The interesting thing was that in all of that dark and reprobate consciousness that so permeated the environment, filled the air, it became common. A person became anesthetized to it. Even the screams in the night of a young man being robbed of his pride and made into a plaything only evoked responses like:

"Shut up, down there, we're trying to sleep!"

How had I come to a place in my life where I could actually be comfortable in that world? Was it resignation? Was it acceptance of the fact that I was doomed to live a life of by-the-hour motels on the streets where the whores strolled and the dealers lurked? Where the gutter held the evidence of the lives that walked those streets—used condoms, discarded syringes, and castoff empty short-dog bottles with names like Thunderbird and Night Train?

What was it in me that had found a way to get comfortable in the backseat of a cop car with my hands cuffed behind my back? I went through the booking process by rote and knew every hallway and vestibule in the jail. Not one bit of it alarmed me or even made me uneasy.

The fact was that I was completely comfortable in that sick and twisted world, and I felt like a captured bird at this table of good, God-loving people. I knew exactly how to conduct myself at a table in a chow hall full of felons and drug addicts, but I was more than apprehensive at a table full of Christians. Something was dreadfully wrong with the picture. As Shakespeare wrote in *Hamlet*:

"Something is rotten in the state of Denmark."

That shepherd's pie was the first home-cooked meal I had had in a very, very long time and I thought:

Jesus calls Himself the Good Shepherd. How apropos.

"So Eddie, do you surf?"

"It's been a while."

"Ever surf Salt Creek?"

"I used to surf Salt Creek when there was just a dirt road down to the point and there were two old men—twin brothers, actually—who had a little travel trailer on the road. It was up on a wood platform and it had a porch on it. One of those brothers would always be sitting there with a long pole that had a clothespin on the end of it. To get by you had to put a dollar on the clothespin."

"Yeah, I heard about that!"

It was Ernie speaking. Ernie was a Chicano-looking dude, short and really broad across the shoulders. All these guys were hair farmers and like Craig, Ernie's hair was curly and hung to his shoulders, the difference being that Ernie's hair was so black it was blue, reminding me at once of my childhood friend in Puerto Vallarta, Vicente. Like Craig there was a luminescence coming off of Ernie. Almost as if when he smiled there was a little sparkle of light, a little shooting star kind of flash, and a quiet little tinkling of bells. It was kind of freakin' me out a bit.

"We got extra boards and the water is really warming up early for June. We're going to dawn patrol. If you want, we can pick you up."

"I'll let ya know before we all split tonight, okay?"

"Yeah, Praise the Lord, bro!"

"*Praise the Lord.*"

I said it to myself, silently, just to see what it felt like. It felt wonderful and all of a sudden I was crying. Right in front of twelve strangers, huge water-balloon-sized tears just jumped out of me. Almost as if they were operating by some word spoken to all of them simultaneously they all got up and gathered around me. I felt hands gently touching my shoulders and my head.

Rich began to pray:

"Lord, mighty God, still Eddie's heart right now and breathe life into him. We don't know what he has been through but You do. You have seen every moment of his life from even before he had life. You know every hurt, every wound, and even every love that Eddie has ever had or ever lost. Please, dear God, make Yourself real to Eddie right now. Invade his heart and his mind with Your Holy Spirit and Your peace. Let tonight be the beginning of a brand-new life, a brand-new adventure. You say in Your Word that if any man is in Christ he is a new creation, old things have passed away and all things become new."

I was being flooded with the very things that Rich was praying for me and the tears were a cleansing river flowing out of me and soaking the front of my Towncraft T-shirt. I was desperately afraid of God right at that moment. Not the kind of fear that makes you want to run but rather a kind of fear that made me want to climb up under the shelter of His wings. It was the kind of fear a kid should have for a loving and just father. It was awe, really, it was reverence. As the tears flowed out God's love flowed in and I felt a renewal, a fresh wind blowing into me. Proverbs, chapter three says:

"Fear the Lord and depart from evil. It will be health to your flesh, and strength to your bones."

I felt health invading my body, my flesh. It was the health of purity, of cleanliness. I felt the strength of righteousness in my bones—not any righteousness of my own, but as the scriptures say in Philippians, chapter one:

"Being filled with the fruits of righteousness which are by Jesus Christ, to the glory and praise of God."

Rich's wife Candy began to pray:

"Dear Lord, thank You for bringing Eddie here to us tonight. I believe You have always directed his path and guarded him as You prepared him for works that he is to do for Your kingdom. All of the darkness and pain that Eddie has lived will be a beacon of light to broken people everywhere once it is transformed into a glorious testimony of your grace."

Rich's wife was a very beautiful woman and her voice was like honey over me. When I say she was beautiful I don't mean in a purely physical sense, although she was very pretty; it was more that she was beautiful because she was truly holy. Not religious or pretentious but humbly holy, in love with God and by extension in love with His people. It reminded me of a passage from First Peter:

"Do not let your adornment be merely outward—arranging the hair, wearing gold, or putting on fine apparel—rather let it be the hidden person of the heart, with the incorruptible beauty of a gentle and quiet spirit, which is very precious in the sight of God."

She continued to pray.

"Oh Lord, please move mightily in Eddie's life. Eddie, have you ever asked Jesus to forgive you of your sins and be your Savior?"

I could only nod and cry.

"But it's been quite a while and you got lost, right?"

More nodding and crying.

"Eddie, do you want to renew your relationship with Jesus?"

Just the sound of that name "Jesus"…when she said it, it held so much hope. It was the most beautiful name I had ever heard. I nodded and still I cried.

"Okay Eddie, Jesus said, 'Behold I stand at the door and knock, and if any man hear me and open the door I will come into him and have fellowship with him and he with Me.' Do you want to open the door, Eddie?"

I managed a yes.

"Okay, say this prayer with me."

She led me in a prayer in which I acknowledged,—no, I fully and tearfully confessed that I was a sinner of great magnitude. This confession erupted out of me, yanked out by the overpowering presence of God's Holy Spirit confirming the truth of my condition. She led me in a prayer asking Jesus to forgive me and to be my Lord, and in that prayer I knew that every Word of the Bible was true, that every heart in that house was true, and I knew down to the marrow of my bones that I was saved.

"Oh man, that was sooo heavy! God is really good!"

"Yes, Craig, indeed He is. Let's clear the table and move to the living room and get into some worship and the Word."

Rich stood up and began clearing the table and Leslie, Rod, and Gary retrieved guitar cases from the hallway and went to the living room. After we got the dishes rinsed and stacked in the dishwasher we headed in to join what I assumed would be the band. Rich put his arm around his wife and I was hit with the revelation that this is what God wanted from us. He wanted us to love Him and spend time with Him. He wanted us to worship Him and He wanted us to do it together, husbands and wives, brothers and friends, sons and daughters. Leslie was a true gift and her singing and playing, accompanied by Rod and Gary on their guitars, opened up the ceiling of that place and gave us access to the very throne room of God.

That night I was transformed and I left there with more hope than I had ever had. Craig and Leslie and I stood outside under the stars for a while after everyone had left.

"How do you feel, bro?"

"I feel really good. Complete, I think."

"You are one of us now and we stay plugged in. We stay right under the spout where the glory comes out. The Bible says that the devil is like a roaring lion roaming to and fro throughout the earth, seeking whom he may devour. I think that holds especially true of Christians. The devil gets really angry when he gets beat and you just beat the devil. We're all going to church for a concert tomorrow night—you need to come with us."

"Where is it?"

"Up in Costa Mesa. It's called Calvary Chapel and it's where all the Jesus people go."

"Jesus people?"

"Yeah, bro, you'll see. It is absolutely amazing. Hey, man, we're gonna take off. You gonna surf in the a.m.?"

"What time?"

"We'll pick you up at five thirty."

"I'll be ready."

Craig and Leslie both threw their arms around me and Leslie quietly spoke to God:

"Lord, bless my new friend and let the seeds planted in him tonight grow into a mighty tree, and make it bring forth lots of sweet fruit."

I watched them walk away and I heard them laughing at some private thing as they got in Craig's truck, and I felt content. But as I turned up the street toward my folks' house I felt a cold wind blow across my spine and I knew it was the breath of demons. I prayed a little prayer of my own:

"Oh God, please help me."

They had owned me for a lifetime and they weren't done with me yet. They weren't going to give me up without a fight. I knew there was going to be a battle and I also knew that my life would be the battleground. I was suddenly aware of a smell that I couldn't quite identify. It smelled a little like ammonia, a little like jail food, and a little like the sulfur smell of a bunch of matches under a spoon of cooking heroin. Or maybe it was brimstone. With that smell came a deep sense of unrest, unease. My hands and feet felt a little numb and my tongue grew thick in my mouth. There was a deathly rotten and yet oddly medicine-like taste in my mouth and a vibration in my bones that was caused by the hungry teeth of my past, gnawing, chewing, trying to suck the marrow out, trying to suck this new life out of me. It all came upon me when I felt that wind, that demon's breath.

"You think you can have the life these people have? You can't have this life. You know where your life is going, don't kid yourself. You have always been mine and you'll always be mine."

I looked up at the sky and I shrugged my shoulders at the moon.

"I don't really give a rip, anyway."

Yeah, the devil thought he had me, and evidently God wanted me and I wanted Him, but I had my walls either way. I had my fortress with ramparts I had been building for a lifetime. The battle might be raging on, forces might be laying siege, but these walls were thick and high.

"Do what you like," I said to the stars, "I am going to sleep."

Only I didn't sleep—no, not at all. I lay there loving and then hating, conquering and then being paralyzed by fear and impending doom. Soaring to the heavens and then burning in a lake of fire. I was the fraying rope in a tug-of-war between good and evil, between God and Satan, and finally the dawn began to purple-up the eastern sky. I got out of bed certain I could never do this thing. I had fallen for all of those people at the Richards' Bible Study, I had fallen into the sweetness of all of it. But man, it was a monumental exercise in futility. It was really a big cosmic joke. I was way too broken. As soon as they found out who I really was they would run. If I shared the things I thought, if I shared the way things looked to me they would be scared away. At that point coffee seemed like the only logical thing. I was leaving the room and something made me turn back. I found myself on my knees by the bed.

"Oh God, can you really save me?"

I didn't hear anything but I felt Something, and that Something said: *"Just go surf and have a good time, tonight I'm going to show you new things."*

I drank a couple of cups, slammed a bowl of shredded wheat, and just as I was rinsing my bowl Craig's headlights washed across the sidelights of the front door. When I opened it they were standing there glowing: Craig and Leslie and...well, God. Yeah, they had Him right there with them; I could feel Him coming off of those two like rays of sunlight punching through the clouds right after a downpour. Craig was holding a pair of Quiksilver trunks out toward me.

"These should fit pretty good. You got a towel?"

Leslie had her guitar and she played and sang for the entire half-hour ride to Salt Creek. In spite of me, my apprehensions were slipping away. This could be what Craig meant when he said:

"You are one of us now and we stay plugged in. We stay right under the spout where the glory comes out."

Ernie, Gary, Larry, and Rod were already in the water and in the line-up at the point. Craig had brought a seven-six, single-fin Parrish Bolt for me. I had a feeling it was his special board. It worked like magic and I was surfing as well as ever after a half hour. Being young is like that. Nowadays if I don't surf for a month I am a total nine ball.

"Hey, bro," Ernie said, "how come now that you have a girlfriend you are the last in the water and the first to leave?"

"I dunno, how come you are too much of a caveman to get a girl-friend?"

"Oh man, I could have a girlfriend; I'm just trying to stay focused on serving the Lord."

That brought laughs all around.

Pretty cool. Pretty normal. We traded waves all morning. From time to time I would look up on the beach to see Leslie playing her guitar to a small crowd or talking to them between songs. We surfed for four hours until we all got hungry.

"Man, let's go grind!"

Larry produced a huge ice chest out of his truck and it was packed with the surfer essentials. It held two loaves of bread, a mammoth jar of Skippy, an equally huge jar of Welch's grape jelly, and three half gallons of milk. PB&J never tasted so good.

"I got at least five people coming to church tonight, guys."

I have to say I would go anywhere Leslie asked me to, maybe even Baker or Needles. She was sparkly. Curly, long, long brown hair with sun kisses all through it and huge, I mean huge bright blue eyes. When she smiled stuff fell off shelves and things fell over. And the thing of it was that it was most assuredly, most definitely a God thing. She had God coming out of her from every pore. You couldn't even look at her with any kind of lustful thoughts. If you did you would probably be struck dead by a light-ning bolt.

"You comin' with us tonight, Eddie?"

"Yeah, Leslie, I think I am."

She smiled at Craig conspiratorially, winked, and said:

"Eddie, tonight is going to blow your mind!"

CHAPTER 4

I was gonna ride the Panhead but Craig and Leslie wanted to pick me up and so about six thirty we were headed up the 405 freeway toward Costa Mesa. We got off the freeway at Fairview, hung a right, and a couple of seconds later we were pulling in to the parking lot of Calvary Chapel Costa Mesa. The sight that greeted me there was like a reunion of all the hippies from Taco Bell on the Coast highway in Laguna, circa 1967. Taco Bell had been the epicenter for the hippie community in Laguna at that time and trust me, the hippie community was huge.

The scene in the parking lot at the church looked just like the scene there in Laguna, only I didn't smell any weed and all of these hair farmers were carrying Bibles. We made our way into the main sanctuary and I actually did see a couple of familiar faces from back in the day on Woodland Drive. Refugees from the Orange Sunshine Generation. Their seeking had finally brought them to the truth. I had arrived at the same truth, though our paths had diverged markedly since the days when I was an acid-soaked hippie kid running around the canyon, slinging pounds of sinsemilla and smuggling packages of heroin across the border posing as the loving grandson of a harmless elderly lady. We walked a lot of dope across at T.J. just lying in the bottom of a shopping bag full of trinkets. We really did look like some old woman and her grandson just out for the tourist stroll, only grandma was a forty-year-old junkie with a gray wig, a scarf, and some support hose. We were good, though. We made that run twice a week for over a year and never once got stopped.

We walked down the aisle toward the front where Ernie was standing talking to some guys. On the stage the band was fooling around with their instruments and I watched as a huge man with a mane of long, wavy dark hair came out from the backstage wings and took a seat at the bench in front of the keyboards.

Ernie and the boys had saved us seats right up front and the ribbing about Craig always being late since he got a girlfriend started immediately.

"You guys don't think I'm worth waiting for?"

"Yeah, Les, you? Definitely. This guy? I don't know. What do you guys think?"

Just then that huge man cleared his throat and said in the most unlikely voice:

"Praise the Lord! Are you all here because you love Jesus?"

A crescendo erupted from the room, as if on cue everyone had found a seat with some folks seated on the floor in front of the stage. The reason all of these long-haired, patchouli-smelling, incense-burning, ex–dope smoking and ex-fornicating castaways were here was because of a man named Pastor Chuck Smith and his wife Kay. After seventeen years of ministerial frustration, Pastor Chuck read a commentary on the book of Romans by a fellow named G. Campbell Morgan and his concept of grace had forever changed. He began teaching out of the book of Romans and at the same time he and Kay had begun to have a burden for the hippie generation that they saw on the streets of Huntington Beach. They opened up their home to these people and they began to get saved. The sanctuary at Calvary was new and had recently replaced the huge tent that had preceded it.

The legend has it that the staunch old blue-haired folks in the congregation were very worried that all of these hippies with their dirty bare feet were going to get the new carpet all soiled. Pastor Chuck either tore out that carpet or threatened to, I don't recall which, but the upshot of it was that the hippies were there to stay. Literally thousands of lives were changed in the next few years and men who came to Chuck's church, barely able to speak they were so tore back from drugs, went on to preach the gospel and start churches of their own. God has moved mightily in the Calvary Chapel family for over forty years. Myself, I would be dead were it not for that man's faithfulness to God.

Back to the big man.

"If you are here tonight and you aren't in love with Jesus, by the end of tonight you will be! It is no accident you are here, you can believe that! God Himself brought you here tonight to meet His son and so I want to help make that introduction. Let's all pray right now, shall we?"

That crescendo of assents again, only louder this time.

"Oh heavenly Father, You are amazing! Your tender mercies are fresh every morning. You are faithful to make a way before us and we love You, Lord. Please speak to us tonight as we worship You in song and hear Your precious Word spoken into us. Please send Your Holy Spirit to fill this place. That He would convict the sinner and show him his need for a Savior and that He would heal the sick, cast out the agents of darkness and set the captives free! In Jesus's name we pray, amen."

Then Big Bill Sprouse and his band The Road Home played a song that forty years later I still sing when I walk before dawn praying and singing to the Lord. Bill's voice was high and sweet, which was unexpected since he weighed around five hundred pounds. Kind of like, Israel "Bruddah Iz" Kamakawiwo'ole. He had the voice of an angel and when he sang these words from King David's fifth psalm, the Holy Spirit stirred grace and mercy, passion and fire into that room full of saints:

"Give ear to my words, O Lord, consider my meditation.

Hearken unto the voice of my cry, my King and my God, for to You I will pray.

My voice You shall hear in the morning, O Lord;

In the morning I will direct my prayer unto You and I will look up."

Bill led the congregation in worshipping the Lord for a long time but it never got tiring. Each song just seemed to open up the atmosphere more and more to God. With each song the dirt that clung to us from the world seemed to be rinsed off of us—at least off of me, but I knew what was happening to me was a corporate thing. We were all in it, and we were in it together. I felt hands slipping into mine from both sides. To my right it was Leslie, but to my left was some girl I didn't know. Everyone in that place just grabbed the hand of the person next to them without prompting. Well, without being prompted by man but rather moved by the Holy Spirit. When the music finally ended a man came out to the pulpit. With his huge Afro and beard, this man looked like he should have been smoking hash from that big, old table pipe at the Red House in Dodge City, but he was carrying a Bible and I was sure this cat had not been stoned in a very long while. He smiled and said:

"Hi guys, let's turn to First Peter, chapter two, starting in verse one."

He read beautifully, clear and rich, giving all the majesty to the scriptures that they should receive.

"Therefore, laying aside all malice, all deceit, hypocrisy, envy, and all evil speaking, as newborn babes, desire the pure milk of the word, that you may grow thereby, if indeed you have tasted that the Lord is gracious."

He preached on those three verses for forty-five minutes and I had never, ever heard anything like it. It never occurred to me that what he was saying wasn't the truth. It had so much veracity, so much power. Here was a man who believed every word that was written in that Holy Book and consequently he preached with authority, conviction, and passion. I was blown away. I felt as if the message was given especially for me. Spoken directly to me, to cause me to desire the pure milk of the Word. The Lord knew I had plenty of malice and treacherous deceit stored up in my heart, and that it was going to take something seriously pure to ferret all that poison out of me. Life had scarred me from a very young age and I had learned early on from being molested repeatedly by a man who had been a trusted and loved mentor that there was very little good in this world. Everyone I had ever loved had been snatched out of my life or they had turned on me. As I listened to him speak I wanted so desperately to buy in. I wanted this transformation. Even at eighteen years old I was tired. All of this felt so good, so true, and yet there was this part of me that seemed to have always been there. It was a part of me that said:

"But don't you know? Kid, you are different, you don't belong here. Look around you, these could never be your people. You are dark and broken, tainted beyond repair. You might polish up for a minute but you are tarnished to the deepest part of your soul."

And then I was crying again, and I thought:

What can I do? I can only hang on and pray and try to read this amazing book. I can only fake it till I make it, or I don't.

Then I saw Him again, hanging bloodied and beaten on that stained and brutal cross, and He lifted His head. I didn't have to hear Him but as I watched Him look my way, I saw His lips utter those words:

"I love you, my child, and I will always be with you."

The first time I had heard Him say those words I was seven years old and right in the middle of the year when I was torn and battered in secret places, young and vulnerable places, just to satisfy the perversions of a sick and twisted demon who presented himself to the world as a good man. Yeah, maybe the voices were right; maybe I was dark and broken and tainted beyond repair.

Through that entire spring and summer I was with Craig and Leslie every day. Craig got me a job as a carpenter's helper on his job. He was a journeyman carpenter and made really good coin. For that matter I made really good coin. We surfed every day after work and I had sought out Mike Armstrong, that old friend of mine who ripped Brooks Street so beautifully as a kid, and had him shape me a board. It was a magic stick. We called it the Sea Poop because, and I don't know why, I had him make it brown, the exact right shade of brown to earn it that moniker. That part was unintentional, I assure you.

I surfed better that summer on that board than I ever had before, maybe not since, but that could be debatable; I'm not sure. When we weren't working or surfing we were in church. I began to forget who I was. I barely rode the Panhead except to keep the pipes blown out, once a week down the road and back, and never at night. That is, until one night about mid-September.

It was one of those nights; there was just something in the air. It had blown in with the Santa Ana winds that came hot and lusty out of the desert. I had just gotten my biggest paycheck yet. It had a bonus attached to it that we got for finishing a job under time and under budget. It was quite a bit of cash—enough so that with four hundreds in the middle and the rest all in twenties and rolled up tight, it made a pretty big bulge in my jeans.

I told Craig and Leslie I would meet them at church, it was too beautiful of a night to be in a car. Only I didn't go to church. I rode up the 55 to the 22 west and headed toward Garden Grove. When I got to the North Main Street exit I pulled over, shut the bike down on the shoulder, and just listened. I was listening for thunder. I was listening for another motor like mine to lead me into the mischief that we all knew would eventually find me. Who was I trying to kid? I was a foreigner in that church crowd. I felt like a stinkin' science project. When Leslie said I should quit slicking my hair back and start looking like a surfer instead of a convict, it kind of crept up on me again. That knowledge that I was not really a part of the group lodged itself in my mind. I waited for about five and then fired up and did the same thing again at The City Drive. This time it wasn't three minutes before I heard at least two bikes coming down the freeway from the same direction I had just come.

They blew by me like a freight train and I fired it up and got after 'em lickety-split. They must have been doing a hundred plus because it's a couple of miles from The City Drive exit to the Harbor Boulevard exit, which is where I caught up with them. My '54 Pan had a ninety-three-inch S&S Sidewinder motor and it would get up and get after it, but if they hadn't slowed down to get off the freeway I don't know how far it would have taken me to catch 'em. There were four of them and they were all patch holders in the same club whose run I would be leaving years later, when I spied the talking dragon that caused me to ride my bike off a twenty-foot embankment.

I couldn't tell if I knew any of them but I was going wherever they were going, that was for sure. We rode surface streets and after a couple of blocks of me following them one of the brothers dropped back to I.D. me. It was a brother named Rabbit.

"Oh, hey, Youngblood, where you headed?"

"Wherever you guys are headed, if that's cool."

He shrugged his shoulders and hollered back:

"Sure, man, come on along. We're going over to the Outpost to see what's shakin' out."

I just nodded my affirmative and he grabbed a handful of throttle to reclaim his place in their little pack. Club guys ride tight. Handgrip to handgrip and tire to tire. I hung back a little, which is the proper etiquette for a guest in the pack. To ride right on up tight with the pack could be taken as a presumptuous move, like you think you're part of something you're not. In all of my years of riding in an outlaw club there is one particular thing that I always found to be in very poor taste: people on the periphery who don't have the heart to do what it takes to earn and keep a patch acting like because they are wearing a support shirt or the same color bandana as the club's colors, they can act like they are a part of. I never liked the whole support-shirt thing. I mean, yeah, it's a way for the club to make money, but those shirts cause people to put on airs. If you aren't in the club, nothin' about the club should ever be comin' out of your mouth. In fact, until you've had that patch for a few years you still should be seen and not heard. It seems to me, as I tally up my memories, that a good bit of the trouble I ever saw clubs get in with each other, or even the civilian biker population, was the result of some hang-around or brand-new guy shooting his mouth off.

We pulled into the Outpost parking lot and I noticed two of the brothers were flying Nevada bottom rockers. I didn't know either of them but the other two I had known since I was fourteen. Both were Mother Chapter OC, Rabbit and Tombstone. Rabbit hugged me and Tom B. punched me in the chest.

"What kind of bird don't fly, Youngblood?"

"Yeah, yeah I know, a jailbird. Hardy-har-har. Everybody wants to be a comedian."

I wouldn't have spoken to Rabbit like that in front of more brothers than this, but the air was light so I knew it was cool. Besides, it had been my first real jail time and I felt kind of qualified.

One of the Nevada brothers said:

"So is that yer name? Youngblood?"

"Nah, my name is Eddie. Rabbit just calls me that 'cuz I'm eighteen and I've been hangin' around since I was fourteen."

"Yer only eighteen? Kid you could end up bein' a monster. I think I'm gonna be nice to you! My name is Whip and this is Kelly."

"Nice to meet you guys."

Brother handshakes all around.

There were probably thirty or forty bikes backed up to the wall, glistening in the neon light of the street night. There were bikers standing in little groups smoking herb or passing pints back and forth. The club guys were off to the side in an exclusive little group, not really fraternizing with the civilians. One of the guys from the new club in the Southland came up to pay his respects to Tom B. Tom was subdued, maybe aloof. A much bigger dog from a much bigger pack.

The women were hard and hip. Shape-fitting leathers, Levis, and boots, some with a knife sheath down their leg. Occasionally you would see one of them laugh or toss a smile out and there would be a softness, but not much and not often. They were posing, playing the role.

"We are hard women running with hard men."

The parking lot was cool but the front door of the bar was beckoning with its cigarette smoke and loud jukebox music pouring out into the night. It was the time of the country outlaw—Willie and Waylon and the boys. The song, "Mamas Don't Let Your Babies Grow Up to be Cowboys," was a favorite, only the scooter folks would change it to "Bikers": "Mamas, don't let your babies grow up to be bikers!" Everyone would sing it and then everyone would laugh and clank beer mugs. Pretty funny, really.

As I walked through the door into the moist heat of a roomful of drunk, wired, unruly heathens I felt a sense of belonging that had been missing since I got out of jail. The familiar and comforting smells of cigarettes, weed, beer, urine, and puke washed over me like a soft, warm, down comforter on a winter night; I snuggled in. This was home, this was where I belonged. I went up to the bar and ordered a pitcher and when I whipped out my roll the dirtbag next to me started sizing me up. He could see I was young. I slid over and whispered in his ear:

"You keep it up and I might get edgy and go right up in ya with this."

I pulled my leather back to reveal my straight-blade Schrade sheathed at my waist.

"Nah, bro, we're cool."

I filled his mug and suddenly realized I was humming along with the jukebox. David Allan Coe.

"And I'll hang around as long as you will let me,
And I never minded standin' in the rain,
But you don't have to call me darlin', darlin',
You never even called me by my name."

Oh man, but I was feelin' fine! The guy I had set straight, kiboshing any notion he might have had about following me to the head and taking my roll, made an introduction. He stuck out a huge gloved paw.

"Duncan. Sometimes they call me Drunk Duncan."

"Eddie. And those guys call me Youngblood."

I nodded toward the brothers who had commandeered a table on the edge of the dance floor.

"You with that crew?"

He sort of tried to get a look at my back.

"They're just friends."

"Well, 'Youngblood'—I like that, it fits you. Anyway, they may call me Drunk Duncan and they'd be speakin' a truth, but I got something right here that no matter how drunk we get will keep us ridin' the line straight and true!"

Duncan held up a black thirty-five-millimeter film can and gave it a shake.

"You up for a little toot, 'blood?"

"It would be splendid, my inebriated compadre!"

We laughed and he nodded toward the knife I had threatened him with just moments before.

"Let's put a pile or two on that blade then, shall we?"

He set the container down on the bar and held out his hand.

"May I show you what I feel might be an appropriate dosage?"

I handed him my Schrade.

"Aha! Who has the knife now, Youngblood?"

He laughed from down in his gut and dipped that blade in the gag. It emerged with at least a teaspoon on it.

"Don't bother if it ain't gonna tickle yer ticker, I always say!"

I hadn't done any crank in almost a year, and in about ten minutes it hit me like a battering ram. But it was a velvet battering ram. It felt so good, everything came alive and got triple-chrome-plated. The girls got prettier, the music got better, the whiskey was sweeter. The bar took on a rhythmic pulsing like a huge heart. It just didn't enter my mind that it was the devil's heartbeat and that I had fallen one more time into a trap he laid for me many years before.

I bought a pack of Camel straights from the machine and stepped outside for a smoke. Leaving the thick, hot air of the bar and stepping outside into the late summer night brought out a deep need in me. The Santa Ana winds were blowing and in their wings they carried a calling. It was a stirring, primal and deep in me, and it was beckoning me to ride the Canyons, taste the pockets of pungent dampness as I hurtled by a creek or stream. I needed to feel the chill of the canyon bottoms and then the summer-night warmth of the ridge tops. I walked over to the Panhead and brushed my hand over its sleekness. Henry Ford said:

"You can paint it whatever color you want as long as it's black."

My sentiments exactly. I thought about how I came into possession of that Panhead. I had inherited Wayne's black 1948 Triumph. Hope had given it to me not long after we had gotten back from putting Wayne's ashes on the reef at Honolua Bay on Maui. I was only thirteen but I rode that bike like a jockey rides a thoroughbred. South Laguna was unincorporated, which meant that there was very little law enforcement—a deputy sheriff here and there, but not much police presence.

I was at the Gulf gas station buying, I think it was twelve cents a gallon, gas and this guy in a pickup pulled alongside me. I recognized him. It was Chuck Vivino. His son was in my grade and was always getting picked on because he was seriously light in the loafers.

"Yer Eddie, right?"

"Yeah, Mr. Vivino. It's nice to meet you, sir."

He raised his eyebrows like he was surprised by my politeness. It was my grandmother's doing. She taught me the value of respect.

"Billy says yer one of the only guys that treats him good."

"Billy's totally cool, Mr. Vivino."

I don't think he ever heard that before.

"You almost done here? I want you to follow me up to my house. I want to show you something."

"'Sure, I'll follow you."

We pulled into his driveway and he got out of the truck. He was wearing engineer boots, 501s cuffed Folsom style, and a white T-shirt with a pack of Camels rolled up in the sleeve. He was a totally '50s bobber-style biker. This was unusual for South Laguna and I wondered why I had never seen him before.

"Have you been away, Mr. Vivino?"

"Merchant marines, son, I'm shipped out most of the time. I don't get to spend much time with Billy and I blame myself for him being the... well, you know, the way he is."

"Sir, Billy would be Billy even if you were with him every day, but just because he's different doesn't mean he's not cool. When I see kids jackin' him around I go ballistic. We don't hang out that much but I would say Billy is my friend. He's smart and wickedly funny. Just give him a chance."

Chuck Vivino looked at me with dawn in his eyes. I could tell he thought I was a cool kid and if I thought his for-sure-gonna-be-way-gay son was cool, then he probably needed to reevaluate. He was getting a little misty around the edges.

"Wow! Thanks, Eddie, I mean it. I knew I was right to bring you up here. Check this out."

He flung open the garage door and there was another tarp. Looked just like the one that covered Wayne's Triumph when I had first seen it over a year ago now. Only thing was, whatever was under it was bigger, way bigger...Chuck Vivino lovingly rolled that tarp back and revealed a chopped and bobbed 1954 Panhead that caused my knees to go weak and my mouth to go dry. What was he showing me this for? He saw me looking curiously at the front end.

"Yeah, different, huh? It's off an Ariel Square Four. That Ariel is a really heavy bike, and that front end on this bike works like a dream."

My eyes slowly went from the front axle to the back axle, missing nothing. I called out my observations.

"Chrome frame, mustang tank, Linkert M74B carb, battery points ignition, the new wiring makes me think it's been converted to twelve volt, mechanical brakes front and rear, fishtail upsweep pipes, and oh, a suicide shifter."

"You know a lot for a kid."

"I do all the work on that Trumpet and I read a lot."

"You want it?"

I laughed at his joke. Of course I wanted it, this guy was too funny.

"What are you talking about?"

"I was saving it for Billy, but we both know he's never gonna want this bike. You, on the other hand, love bikes and I know from what I've heard from Billy you've got heart, courage, and hustle. Eight hundred bucks. You can take the bike and have six months to pay."

I thought I was gonna pass out. I put my hand out and said:

"Mr. Vivino, you have got yourself a deal!"

"Good, but just call me Chuck, okay? Mr. Vivino was my father."

"Okay, Chuck, but I gotta tell you I am in shock and disbelief."

"Yeah, me too, kid, but let's roll it out. You gotta ride it out of here today or I might change my mind."

It took a little doing and one fall,—I made sure I was between the bike and the pavement—to get used to the foot clutch and hand shift, but by the time I got to Hope's I pretty much had it down. I rapped those fishtails from the street and Hope came out on the deck. She had a big smile on her face when she saw me on the Pan.

"I know why you're here, young Edward. Go ahead, sell the Triumph. You should have Chuck's bike."

So they had already talked. She knew I'd come straight here to check things out with her and so did he. I loved her for her way with me. Now I could sell Wayne's bike to help pay off Chuck. I spoke into the wind:

"I hope it's cool with you, Wayne-o."

CHAPTER 5

Here I was, five years later, wired out of my mind, standing next to that same '54 Pan in the parking lot of a biker bar in Garden Grove. Oh, that bike had gone through a lot of changes. I had changed out the mustang tank for a set of three and a half gallon Harley fat bob tanks. I had replaced the front end with a UL Springer. I had a mini Hallcraft disc brake in the front. I had made the motor into a monster and ditched the stock Linkert carb for a Weber and the battery points ignition for a magneto. I kept the fishtails. It was all black and chrome and it was scary fast. Now it was time to scare myself. I'm joking; nothing about 100 miles an hour scared me. It was at that kind of speed that I could catch up with myself. A hundred miles an hour seemed just right to me. I knew exactly where I was going, but first I headed back into the bar to see if I could purchase a little of that go-fast from Drunk Duncan or one of the brothers. I wanted a little doggie bag, so to speak. Duncan had disappeared, but I could see Rabbit was chewing the inside of his face so it was very likely that he had the goods.

"Hey, Rabbit, can I talk to you for a sec?"

"Sure, Youngblood, what's up?"

"The wind, it's almost hot out tonight. I'm a little wired and I need to go for a ride through the hills. I was wondering if you had any crank I could buy for the road."

He got a mischievous grin, kind of cocked his head to one side like he was trying to see me from a different perspective.

"Go to the bar, get the phone book from the barkeep, tear out a page for a bindle, and meet me in the head."

I went in the head, and he was waiting. It was just me and him in there. I tore the page down a bit, folded it into a bindle, and handed it to Rabbit.

"You know I'm only doin' this 'cause you're eighteen now and can make your own decisions. But what I know about you is that a little ain't never enough and there's no stop in you once you get goin'. Don't make me regret this, little bro."

I was touched by the sentiment of his words but even more by the look in his eye. That was one of the defining moments in my commitment to the biker lifestyle. This hard-riding, hard-drinking and -drugging, extremely dangerous man cared about me. He locked his eyes on my face and he was searching me.

"I know you shoot dope, kid."

In that life being a hype was a big no-no. Man, you could smoke, snort, or eat all the drugs in the stinkin' world and that was all right, but the needle was taboo. That didn't mean people didn't do it; it was just way on the down low. I suddenly knew how he knew and I was surprised that I hadn't been braced for it before this. About a year before, in fact just before I went to jail, Monkey Man had paroled from Lompoc. He had just started prospecting for the club. He had always been a die-hard dope fiend and a serious gangster. He was never really a biker or a club kind of guy. He got around a couple of brothers inside and all that changed. He ended up being one of the most dependable and stand-up patch holders I had ever met. Anyway, when he paroled he was staying with Wrench; I was, as well. He saw me loaded on heroin. A dope fiend can always tell. He asked me to score and so I did. We were in the garage getting ready to fix when Wrench walked in.

"What are you guys doin'?"

Monk answered right up:

"Somethin' you gotta be quiet about if you and me are bros."

"Yeah, fine, but you better have enough for me 'cause if I gotta keep a secret I wanna get paid for it."

We all fixed and the next thing we know Wrench is toppling over like a felled redwood.

"Oh man, he's done gone out on us!"

He was already turning blue. We got him butt naked and started filling the bathtub with ice. It took a while but we brought him around. I knew that either Monk or Wrench had told Rabbit, but apparently that was as far as it had gone.

"I haven't slammed in a year, Rabbit."

"You've been locked up for a year, Eddie."

Suddenly I was Eddie and I knew that it was getting a tad bit more serious. He looked hard at me and then he grabbed me by the shoulders.

"I don't want to bury you, kid, you got way too much potential. You could be somebody—what am I sayin'? You already are somebody! Eighteen years old and hangin' with the big boys. I've seen you stand up after getting knocked down and just keep on comin'. Yer never scared, you ride like the wind, and I trust you. Don't lose that to a needle and a spoon."

Well, don't you know that is exactly what I did, but it took a while. Rabbit pulled a big bag of dope out of his inside pocket and I knew it was the goods. It looked like diamonds. He scooped a couple of grams at least into my bindle. It was so full I had to do a big hit to shrink the pile down enough to get the bindle folded. That blast peeled my cap off almost immediately and I had to get out of there. I couldn't talk, or stand still. I ordered three shots of Jim Beam, slammed 'em down, and headed out. Scooter fired on the first kick, just like always, and I threw that suicide in gear, dumped the clutch, and I was in the wind. I was thankful for the loud fishtails, it made it so I couldn't hear my heart. I thought of what Duncan said:

"Don't bother if it ain't gonna tickle yer ticker, I always say!"

My ticker was way past tickled.

I took the 22 east to the 55 went up to Chapman and headed out Santiago Canyon. I had ridden this road enough so that I knew every nuance of the surface, every curve, every death-fast straightaway. Those pipes were singing to me and the air was fat with late-summer smells: the sun-cooked wheat mixed with sage, the fragrance of the chaparral; the damp coolness and the moldering smell of a body of still water as I raced past Irvine Lake. A big stroker motor ran its best at night and better still after midnight. I had about an hour to go, I guessed.

I hit the Silverado Canyon entrance at about 80 miles an hour and the temperature dropped a good twenty degrees. I felt the chicken skin come up on my arms and I felt alive. The wind was tearing at my cheeks, pummeling my chest, I could feel my jeans whipping against my legs. One hand was down at my left side, resting on the fifty-caliber shell that was my shifter, and the other was twisting the throttle whose cable was connected to a fire-breathing beast of the night. It spewed thunder into the quiet of the canyons and split open the darkness with its roar. A laugh came up out of some deep part of me and went out into the cloud of demons that were flying at my side and laughing as well, only they were laughing at me, not with me. They were laughing because they had now successfully reclaimed my life. Might as well stop at Cook's and drink a little whiskey and a couple of beers.

The parking lot was full of bikes and there was a fight going on in the middle of it all. I stopped to watch for a minute and was amused at the ineffectiveness of the combatants, both windmilling punches that were flying wild. They were gonna wear themselves out, fall down in a heap, and then help each other up, go inside and continue the drunk fest. I didn't know either of them so I walked on by. There was a band doing a Marshall Tucker cover, "24 Hours at a Time," and they were doing it pretty darn well. I walked up and ordered a Jim Beam and a draft from the kind-of-cute bartender, and parked it on a stool. I laid my Camels and my Zippo on the bar and went to the head to do a snout-full of gag. The lift-up door that allowed bartenders ingress and egress from the bar was adjacent to the hallway to the head and as I walked by I got homegirl's attention. I held my forefinger up to the side of my nose in inquiry and she was there in a flash. She slipped into the bathroom with me and asked:

"So what is your name, Sir Galahad?"

"Eddie."

I held a knife blade of go-fast up to her face and as she said:

"Amber."

She blew that pile into the air.

"I'm so sorry. Sheesh, what a dummy."

She was getting cuter by the minute. I would have expected her to drop the F bomb but, "Sheesh, what a dummy!" That kind of raised her up in my estimation. I laughed. I wasn't good with girls, never had been. I'd always been around people a lot older than me and I never really had the time to develop the social niceties one learns going on dates and going to proms and stuff.

"That's okay there's plenty. Let's try again."

She had her hand on mine, to guide it presumably, but our eyes locked and it got deep for a second.

"I gotta get back to the bar, Eddie. Everything is on the house—your money is no stinkin' good here tonight."

"What if I come back tomorrow night?"

"Eddie, do not worry about tomorrow, for tomorrow will worry about its own things. Sufficient for the day is its own trouble."

A chill went up my spine because I had heard this very verse of scripture spoken at church and it had struck me so I memorized it.

"Matthew 6:34."

That gave her cause to pause and look at me in a new light.

"What is this, Eddie? Who are you?"

"Amber, that is a question that has plagued me all of my life."

"Yeah, me too, Eddie. We have a lot to talk about—you want to stick around? We're closing in a couple of hours. The band is all right and the drinks are free to you."

"You have a jacket, Amber?"

"Of course. I might know a couple of Bible verses, but don't think for a minute that yer the first cowboy to wanna take me to the rodeo. I'm always ready for a ride."

She was a contradiction in terms, just like me. The hardness that had emerged in her voice was contradictory to the girl she had been in the head. She had a liveliness in her bright green eyes that gave her a certain beauty, a certain magnetism.

"Yeah, I'll stick around and we can go for a ride but don't get all 'tough biker chick' on me. It doesn't suit you. You are more than that, I can tell."

The band played, I drank, occasionally Amber and I would slip into the head to reenergize, and before long the band was announcing their last song and those words that sound a mournful dirge in the ears of all die-hard booze hounds:

"Last call for alcohol!"

Everyone had left, the band was packing up, and I helped Amber restock the bar. In the course of carrying out her responsibilities we would inadvertently—I think, maybe—brush up against one another and it would be like an electric shock. When we had the place all secured and the padlock was on the beer cooler, the front door bolted tight, I fired up the Pan and she slipped up on the pillion pad behind my solo seat. She put her arms around me tight. All she said was:

"Oh, my!"

I felt it too. We blasted out of there, slingin' gravel and splittin' the night wide open, and she fit back there like she wasn't there. Except she was very much there and I felt stuff I had not really ever felt. We rode fast through the early morning silence, the stillness shattered as we passed the home of John Q. Public tucked safely away in his bed behind doors that held mortgages and taxes, and it seemed to me a ball and chain of drudgery. We rode down Trabuco to El Toro Road and headed toward the ocean on Laguna Canyon.

My spirits began to soar as I drew nearer to the place, the town that was always my cradle. Entering Laguna through the canyon has always brought about a decompression in me. It always causes me to breathe, deeply and fully. Having Amber with me was a new and curious thing, but I sensed that it would be good to share this part of me with her. We stopped at Woodland Drive and I told her about the Brotherhood days, about Stevie, Max, Wayne, and Hope. Then she was in my arms and her lips were on mine and it was spectacular.

I couldn't remember the last time I had kissed a girl but I thought it was probably Lynn Deimer in seventh grade—just before her father barged into her room and threw me out by the scruff of my neck. Like I told you, I was not good with girls. I held Amber for a long time, just feeling the girlness of her. She was soft and she breathed soft. She had a smell, it was almost buried in the smells of the bar, cigarettes and so forth, but it was there and it spoke to a lost and lonely part of me. Her head was on the right side of my chest and her hand was over my heart and for the first time since Michelle, the first innocent love of my prepubescent life, I felt that thing. I also knew that the dawn was going to find me dropping her off at her car back in the parking lot of the bar and that I would more than likely never see her again. Where I was headed there was no room for a soft side, no room for the liability of love. In fact in spite of all that I was feeling I knew that love was a big fat lie. Still, whatever it was that we were doing felt good and I could live with that.

We rode to all my old haunts, we rode by Wayne and Hope's, Philly's and the place where I had stabbed the child molester while coming on to a dose of LSD twenty-five. We parked at the top of the Brooks Street stairs and I told her about learning to surf under the mentorship of Wayne. I told her what had happened to Wayne and how I didn't realize it at the time but Hope died then too. It took a long time for them to bury her, almost three and a half years. When she finally overdosed on heroin she had been reduced to a skeletal, almost toothless, gibbering caricature of the beautiful and intelligent woman she had once been. I had begged and I had pleaded with her but she had set sail for that over-the-horizon place and nothing was going to stop her from pulling up anchor on this world.

When I finished talking about Hope I talked about Michelle and then Faith. These are not the kinds of things one talks about with riding partners or cell mates and frankly I hadn't even known I wanted to talk about 'em. Amber just kind of brought it out of me. I don't know, maybe any pretty girl with her arms around my waist and her head on my chest would have done it, made it all come out.

We kissed again, more slowly and tenderly this time. Kind of weird, I guess, but I was eighteen years old and this was really the first time I had "made out." It kind of freaked me out. I imagine it was because I knew I had someplace I had to be. I didn't have time for these kinds of dalliances. My true love was waiting for me. Yeah, it was time to drop Amber off and get to gettin'.

She was walking toward her car and I was watching her hips sway, probably a little more than they normally would since she knew I was watching. I thought to myself:

Leslie never walked like that, not even once in her life.

"See ya around, Eddie!"

I let my fishtails answer.

The sky was dawning up, purple and lavender going down to marmalade, and I knew that by the time I got there they'd be almost ready to get up. I twisted the wick on that Panhead and grabbed gears till I hit top, then just settled in and let it roll. It was kind of strange how we had that one moment at the bar, the thing with the Bible verse, and we never talked about it again. Probably just as well, I didn't want to think about Craig or Leslie or Jesus. In fact just thinkin' about not thinkin' about all of that made me feel dark and dismal. I pulled over and shoveled a big hit out of my yellow pages bindle and thought it still looked like a couple of grams. Well, good then, I knew just what to do and it was gonna be fun.

The sun was fully up when I rolled up onto the Martinezes' front lawn in Delhi and it was going to be a hot September day. I rapped my pipes before I shut it down and I heard a bunch of cussing coming from behind the curtain in Richard's room. I had met the Martinez family through Max when I was about thirteen, and I had been shooting dope at their kitchen table ever since. There weren't a lot of white guys allowed past the living room hallway. Max and now me, Joey Stapish, Lyin' Louie Carletta, Johnny Primrose, Jimmy Spradlin and maybe the Lupien brothers. If you were runnin' and gunnin' in the OC in the seventies you knew who these guys were.

I just walked in, the front door was always unlocked. No one would ever try to throw down on this house, but if you walked in you sure better be welcome. I went straight for the kitchen. Even a blind man could find the Martinezes' kitchen because that's where grandma Martinez held court and she held court on that big old eight-burner stove and those two big ovens. What needs the uncles, sons, and brothers couldn't provide for by selling heroin she provided selling homemade tamales, tortillas, cakes for quincineras, and the best menudo in Santa Ana.

"*¡Hola, Mijo, dame unos brasos! Donde has estado?*" Hi, mijo, give me a hug! Where have you been?

"*En una adventura, abuelita.*" On an adventure, grandmother.

"*¡Ha ha, mentiroso estavas en el carcel, yo se!*" Ha-ha, liar, you've been in jail, I know!

Richard came into the kitchen in a pair of boxers and slippers.

"Abuelita, leave Eddie alone and cook us up some *huevos revueltos.*"

"How much for a paquete, homie?"

"Three hundred."

I waited for him to wake up a little bit.

"Okay, okay, two fifty."

I just looked at him, thinking he must have forgotten that I muled a whole bunch of his dope across the border and I knew exactly what it cost him to cut it bag it up and put it on the street. He smiled, got up, and poured a cup of coffee. Over his shoulder he said:

"One paquete, fifteen twenty-five-dollar balloons, get out of jail homecoming present. You happy now?"

"Claro que si hombre."

He reached up on top of the cupboard and pulled down a Tupperware container and also got down a rolled bandana that held a cooker and a ten pack of insulin syringes. He tossed me the works and picked out a paquete from what looked like at least a hundred of them.

"A lot of green ones in here, I know you like green."

"Yeah, well, Ricardo let me fix you up a little wake-up hit—out of mine, on me."

"*Ándale pues huero*, now you're talking!"

I pulled the cooker out of the bandana and slipped two brand-new U-100s out of the ten pack that was in there and laid everything out ceremoniously on the table. Abuelita just kept on making breakfast. I snapped a couple of balloons into the spoon and then pulled out my little packet of diamonds. Richard's eyebrows raised but he didn't say anything. Keep in mind this was before the cocaine and heroin speedball came around and I only knew a few junkies who did speed at that time. Being involved in the biker lifestyle, which was fueled by meth, it was only natural that I would test out the synergistic properties of this particular cocktail, I mean, right?

I could see Richard getting apprehensive but I knew he'd go along. There is that machismo thing with these guys. I love that about them. I cooked up the junk, set the cooker down, and poured in a liberal amount of rocket fuel. A few little wisps with the cap end of the outfit and it was cotton time. I peeled a little cotton off one of the Marlboro filters lying on the table and balled it up. Plop, in it went. I drew what looked like half up in the first syringe, then filled the second; a little equalizing and we were set.

"You ready, carnale?"

"*Simon.*"

Richard already had the bandana wrapped around his bicep and was slapping up a vein, so I said:

"Abuelita, will you tie me off?"

Those mahogany-brown and arthritic old hands grabbed hold of my arm strong and sure. We both got a register at the same time and I just slammed mine home. Richard booted his a tad bit, squeezing a little in, pulling back the plunger and flooding the chamber with blood again.

"C'mon, chicken, drive it home! I wanna see your face when it hits you!"

And drive it home he did. Then he jumped promptly up out of his chair and ran out the front door and did some laps around the front yard in his boxers, slippers gone by the wayside.

Abuelita and I cackled like a couple of hens. What was wrong with this picture? Shoot, man, we were family!

CHAPTER 6

A sharp back hand across my chest snapped me back into the present. Stormy.

"Earth to Eddie, earth to Eddie! What the heck, man, you goin' into a coma or somethin'? For somebody who is supposed to be twenty-four hours late for a fix, you sure are relaxed about that outfit in your hand!"

"Oh yeah, I was just thinking."

"Eddie, if you asked me, and Ricky used to say the same thing, and in fact so does Blue, but homeboy, you think way too much. Who knows, maybe someday you can write a book about all that stuff that's clanging around in that head of yours."

"Yeah whatever."

"And Eddie, one more thing."

"What, Storm...?"

"Don't change, ever, 'kay?"

She had leveled out from the rhino shot I had given her and suddenly I realized that I had not really thought about Hope for a while. My little trip down memory lane had brought her memory back and it didn't feel good. In my mind I saw her beautiful and then I saw what became of her as grief and dope took her life. Dope that I gave her. Now I had just given another grieving widow her first speedball. Self-loathing took on dramatically new proportions. Man, there was no comin' back from the pit I had descended into. It was my turn and I hadn't done a shot in over twenty-four hours. I had two rigs, one in my hand, pure speed, and one parked in my lap, all heroin. I took that bandana and made my ropes come up. Storm was watching me curiously.

"Eddie, you are one freaky dope fiend!"

"That's what they tell me."

I took one rig and got it registered, just let it hang and then plugged another one in downstream. I pushed that first one in as fast as I could and the top of my head came off. The second one I just feathered—push a little, pull back and watch the blood rush in, push a little more.

The experience of being at Joseph's should have given me pause, caused me to, I dunno, maybe try to change direction. I had almost been killed in the accident, I saw the life of a man of honor, I relived all of the darkness and pain that had been my upbringing, I had seen that bloody man on that cross who always said to me:

"I love you, my child, and I will always be with you."

I recognized the exact moment when I let go of any hope of ever living a conventional life. It was that tribal moment with Storm and Blue before we left the run. Whatever chain was anchoring me finally rusted through and gave way. Whatever rope had tethered me had finally frayed and broken and I saw the truth.

"Abandon hope, all ye who enter here!"

I had gone past the point of no return and it seemed to me the only road ahead was meant to be ridden at full throttle. I realized I had been holding my breath and it went out in a rush, and with it went any care I had for my life. Bob Seger just kept on singin'.

"He wants to dream like a young man
With the wisdom of an old man.
He wants his home and security.
He wants to live like a sailor at sea.
Beautiful Loser, where you gonna fall?
When you realize, you just can't have it all
You just can't have it all."

Yeah, I had realized all right.

I leaned back against the headrest and adjusted the mirror. Blue was about a hundred feet behind us, doing exactly what I was gonna keep on doing until I stopped breathin'. He was set down real low with one foot draped across his foot peg, just hanging. His left hand was resting on his hand shifter and I knew exactly what he was feeling.

By the time we rolled onto Polk Street in North Highlands I had worked myself into a fury about Jack. It was obvious to me that he had invited Billy and Chris in to his pad as a kind of insurance against me and Blue. He knew he had been trespassing into a forbidden area with Stormy and the tension between us was palpable. He thought Billy and Chris were his homeboys but they knew he had no character and they knew we were for real. They were gonna land on Jack like a starving tick on the neck of a fat dog.

He was so stupid—he thought they would rally against us when in reality they were going to suck him dry and then use him up. They would take every bag of dope he got, all his cash, and I would bet he had already been kicked out of his bedroom and his girlfriend made to stay behind. The thing that really made me angry was the danger he put Stormy and the girls in.

Wherever these guys went there was a good chance of the place busting out in gunfire or a myriad of other dark possibilities.

When Stormy pulled the Ranchero into the driveway and parked I was blind with rage. I hobbled out of the car and up to Jack's door. As I kicked it off the hinges I yelled, "I'm just here for Jack!"

Billy was sitting in Jack's easy chair, watching TV, and I could see down the hallway that Chris was in the bedroom and, just as I thought, Jack's girl was in there with him. As for Jack he was posted up at the bar between the kitchen and the living room with his head in his hands and shoulders all slumped in defeat. It was about to get worse. Billy just nodded at me, made a quick appraisal of my broken condition, and smiled. Chris just kicked the door closed.

Jack tried to get up and run but I was on him like a cheap suit. I had a little pocket knife with a one and a half inch blade and I started burying it in Jack's belly. The blade wasn't long enough to kill him but he didn't know that. I stabbed him ten or twelve times in the front and he turned to run toward the closed and no doubt locked bedroom door. I chased him down the hall, stabbing him repeatedly about the neck and shoulders, being careful to stay away from his spine. Realizing the door was locked when he tried to open it he collapsed against it and slid down to the floor, leaving long smears of bloody streaked handprints.

I almost felt bad for Jack in that moment as he realized that he was a fool for putting this plan in motion. Billy was laughing riotously from his place on Jack's precious throne of a La-Z-Boy. Jack had been duped into thinking that these two men, who were really just like me and Blue, would do what he wanted. He was a fool to think that he could manipulate these hard men into playing his little game by pitting them against me and Blue. Now he was in a sobbing heap on the outside of a locked door that separated him from his own bed and the woman he shared it with.

Yeah, I almost felt bad for Jack for a moment, but then the image of Storm's fear and the weeping she did into my arms rekindled my anger and I suddenly remembered Jack's motorcycle in the garage. Blue had come into the living room and was sitting on the couch, talking with Billy as if nothing unusual at all was going down. I walked past them and through the kitchen door into the garage. Billy was still chuckling.

Rummaging around in Jack's toolbox I found a large ball-peen hammer—a favorite tool of destruction for any task. I commenced working on the bike and I didn't stop swinging that hammer until every square inch of that once pretty Shovelhead was destroyed. It would have been so much more prudent to just make Jack sign over the bike, especially since mine was in pretty poor shape, but the carnal pleasure I was getting out of this was exquisite. This was the ultimate challenge, the ultimate affront to Jack's manhood, second only to what Chris had done by shutting Jack out of his room and keeping Jack's girl in there with him. I was saying:

"Lay down, boy! You can no longer walk among us!"

Finally my own pain and need for a shot caused me to drop the hammer, go to the living room, and plop down next to Blue on the couch. Jack was still curled up by the bedroom door bleeding and whimpering, probably thinking he was going to die at any moment.

"I forgot how much fun it is to watch you when you finally lose it, bro! That was good! Wish we'd had some hot buttered popcorn! Woo-hoo, you be crazy, Dog!"

"Yeah, Blue, I know."

"So you're Eddie, I take it. My name is Billy, and that truly was quite a show! Whaddya say, wanna do a big fat shot on Jack?"

Then we were all laughing.

Jack's by this time almost ex-girlfriend convinced Chris to let her take him to the hospital. I suspect it was in her mind to drop him off at the front door of the ER and burn rubber, shouting out the window:

"Don't come back, worm boy!"

But alas, with ladies you just never know. On the other hand, with dope-fiend ladies you can figure pretty accurately they're gonna go with the guy who can pay the price of the habit, or at least equip them with the means to do it themselves. Once Jack had whimpered his way to the car we all sat down to palaver.

"Man, if I'd of known I was gonna miss all that I would have left the door open. But then there probably would have been a screaming woman, and I just can't take a screaming woman."

Chris was crisp and smart, funny too, and like many career convicts he was very well spoken.

In the pen you either dumb down by succumbing to the baser twisted pathology of the place, or you play what you gotta play when you gotta play it, but you read and you educate yourself.

Your yard time is your politicking and your posturing, your cell time is your true education. It is the time and place when you transcend your past and your present circumstances and you train your mind. You read the philosophers, you read the great fiction kings, you grow a vocabulary, you grow a brain. Chris was poor white trash from Modesto and he was absolutely going to die from this life either in the joint or in some dark midnight escapade, or maybe from AIDS or hep, but I am sure he could carry on very well with a Stanford professor.

Billy and Chris looked at each other and the same kind of unspoken communication that Blue and I had passed between them. They both nodded and Billy spoke first.

"We may have a way to earn some really big money. Chris and I have been working on this plan for the last year but it is going to require two more guys, and lo and behold here you guys are, two of the OC's finest."

"Yes, it is indeed quite fortuitous."

That softened up any remaining tension and also made it clear that, yeah, Chris had been reading.

"We're all ears."

None of us had ever met but I knew that, just as Blue and I had checked into who was who in North Sac and knew all about Chris and Billy, they had done the same and knew exactly who we were and what we could be expected to show an interest in. I was now beginning to wonder if in fact they had come here looking to enlist us, and Jack and his house and his girl were just a convenient little extra bonus. Poor Jack. Maybe someday I would apologize.

"Our adventure begins in a little strip bar called The Pretty Kitty on Auburn Boulevard, just north of Watt Avenue. It is a multifaceted kind of job. First it's a robbery, and then a day or two later it's an arson gig. The owner has four clubs around Nor Cal and on the first and third Fridays of the month all the cash from all four clubs goes through The Kitty. The biggest amount of cash would be on the first Friday, since all the guys on Social Security or welfare are in there spending their monthly dole, so that would be our preferred hit night."

"How much do you figure?"

"At least eighty and possibly a hundred thou."

Blue and I were clear to go back to the OC The kidnapping we had done that caused us to come north had been squashed, and the club had given us the green light to come home. That much of a cash infusion could finance our whole setup. It would also pay to get Stormy out of Sactown and out to Hemet, where she had friends and family that could look out for her and the girls.

"Okay, so why the burn-down after?"

"We were in Folsom with the owner's brother; he's doing life. He approached us almost a year ago about a couple of other little deals just to see how long our reach was. We knew he was checking us out but his cred is right so we went along. Breezy stuff, no biggie.

"Then one day he comes at us and tells us about his brother and his clubs and his business partner. The partner owns thirty percent but he does none of the work and he is a total square. He says it would be really easy to scare him out of the biz for a fraction of his partnership interest if the right people were to make things hard on them."

"The head on this deal, the owner, he doesn't want a cut?" I ask.

"He'll get it on the insurance from the burn."

So then Chris asked the old guy with the deal:

"What do you want for the designs on this thing?"

"I'm old and I'm gonna die in here, I just want some peace. There is someone who is making it hard for me to get any peace and I want him to go away."

"We made him go away and so here we are, and we got a plan."

"Well it's about five o'clock. How about we cruise up there about eleven and look around?"

"Yeah, that will work," Blue said. "It'll give me time to get this knucklehead to the ER and see what's really broken."

"What happened to you anyway?"

I told the whole story and Chris and Billy just listened in rapt amazement. Neither of them rode and neither of them did hallucinogens, so the story of the dragon really freaked them out.

"Man, you guys really are crazy!"

I thought that statement was hysterical coming from a guy like Chris Dalton. He had been cooking up a shot and as he tied off and slipped the rig in the ditch I saw the shamrock tattoo on his forearm: the centerpiece to a collage of demons and lost souls that made up the fine single-needle tattoo work that was a sleeve on his arm. That shamrock identified him as a bona fide member of the Aryan Brotherhood, a white prison gang that demanded a lifetime commitment. Blood in and blood out. I had done a bunch of county time and I had been to prison for three years so far, but Chris and Billy were lifers. Even though they were on the street at that particular moment their real lives were inside. Blue was state raised too, but being a biker somehow separated him from that mentality that guys like Billy and Chris shared.

Blue didn't want to go back, though we all knew each of us would go back. Blue loved to ride and to be free, but Billy and Chris lived for the politics and the action of the prison yard. They felt locked up outside and free inside. On the streets they had nothing but a few moments of intense crime and debauchery, but they felt very much out of place and uncomfortable. In the pen they were in their element and the dangers of negotiating their way through the treacherous microcosm of prison was what they knew and understood.

Deuel Vocational Institute, or Tracy, was nicknamed the Gladiator School because it had been a youth prison at one time where they housed particularly heinous juvenile offenders right alongside adult convicts. At one time a juvenile could receive a sentence of one year to life and would be sent to Tracy. Even after it became an adult facility the name stuck, but the name is telling because in so many ways prison is just like the gladiatorial arena.

Held in cells in cell blocks where deals are made for everything from food to cigarettes, from drugs to sex. In the concrete cell houses where racial hatreds boil and animosities brought on by cultural chasms brew a dark and bitter cup, where a word whispered in the night can easily mean blood spilled in the morning.

Every day these festering boils of hatred are released into an exercise yard to explode in violence. Men like Chris and Billy left their cells in the morning with homemade knives, some ten inches long and called bone crushers, ensconced in orifices in their bodies that were in no way designed for that job. This was the life they understood and this was the life that in some sick and twisted way they loved.

"I'm gonna get Eddie over to the ER. We'll meet you back here about ten o'clock."

"Sounds good, Blue, see ya then."

We walked out of the pad, I headed for the shotgun side of the Ranchero and Blue dropped the trailer. He was just hopping in on the driver's side when Stormy came out of the pad and leaned in the truck.

"Eddie, what did you do to Jack?"

"Oh, what makes you think it was me?"

She gave me that *Oh really, you tryin' to go there right now?* look, but it had this special Storm thing on it that made me adore her. For the first time I was seeing the ravages of Ricky's death and the increasing weight of knowing she was becoming a junkie and it tore her down because she was first and foremost a mom. But she was a mom who had been robbed of her partner and best friend and the spoonful of comfort that was taking his place was trying to make her as dead as her man. The wrestling match of grief and guilt she was engaged in was proving a powerful foe, and I knew we had to get her out of Sactown or she would surely die here.

"I just gave a little less than he probably deserved, but all you need to know is that things with Chris and Billy are jam up and jelly tight. You need to call Jerry and Carmen and tell them you need to find a little house out there in the valley."

"But...But, I..."

I watched as the reality of what I was saying hit her.

With Storm this was a crossroad: her desire to get clean and be a good mom meeting face-to-face with the prospect of leaving the comfort that heroin was providing. That warm blanket of caramel that just made it all go away. The thought of the cold emptiness of withdrawal may have just been as fearful as losing Ricky. It gets that deep of a hold on you.

"Just do it, little sister. This isn't a negotiation."

On her face was a mixture of fear, resignation, and gratitude—and maybe just a faint glimmer of hope.

At the hospital they found that I had two broken bones in my wrist, three broken ribs, and a broken collarbone. They gave me a brace for my collarbone, put a cast on my wrist, and taped up my ribs. They gave me a scrip for Tylenol-Codeine number fours. I asked them for something for sleep and they gave me some Nembutal. It would be a perfect kick pack for Storm once we got her on the road.

CHAPTER 7

Ten o'clock found us sitting at the coffee table, and I laughed inside as I watched Jack's chick wrap herself around Chris like a boa constrictor. I had seen this so many times. A dope-fiend chick will always jump up for the biggest, baddest dog in the pack. There is nothing badder in their minds than the freshly paroled incarnation of emotional unavailability, aloof detachment, danger, and prison-made muscles. It was time to lay out a plan, so he handed her an outfit full of dope and without a word hooked his thumb over his shoulder. She pouted a little but silently got up and went in the bedroom. Chris looked up from under his ball cap–shrouded brow and kind of smiled mischievously, and we all had a little chuckle. All he said was:

"Dumb as a box of rocks, right?"

We took two cars, parked at opposite ends of the joint, and strolled on in separately. Kind of lame, really, when I thought about it later. I mean, we looked like bookends, and what are the odds of two pairs of seriously gangster-looking dudes walking in a place at the same time by chance? Walking in separately almost looked like we were for sure together and up to something. On the other hand, nobody in there probably gave a hoot, and the security probably wouldn't want any of what we had to give 'em.

I hated strip joints. Such a twisted perspective on what was happening and twisted on the parts of all the participants. Guys going in there with a wad of one-dollar bills, thinking that they could be the man, feeling like some kind of underground X-rated kingpin, imagining themselves to be that guy who could get what he wanted with a snap of the fingers. The girls thinking that they had the whole thing in the grip of their ridiculously long acrylic nails, and that all those grease-stained bills folded in half and stuffed in the waistband of their G-strings somehow made them powerful. All of it perpetrated in the barely lit corners on the filth-stained cushions of secluded booths, hands busy under the chipped Formica tabletops. The problem for me with seeing the depravity of such a deep moral bankruptcy was that it so brought it home how morally, spiritually, and emotionally bankrupt *I* was. The truth of it all was that the only one with any game in here was the devil, and he was a puppeteer making all these would-be players dance to his dark dirge.

"Oh God, who am I? Is this all there is for me?"

"Hey, man, you look like a rough ride…"

She was already sitting in my lap.

I scooted out from under her and fished in my pocket for my roll, wincing in pain from collarbone and ribs. I had sawed the cast off as soon as we got back to the pad and I left the brace in the truck. I didn't want anyone to remember a guy with a cast and a brace. I was pretty sure I was done with that brace anyway. There was plenty of dope.

"Oh man, I'm sorry. What happened?"

"I play football for the Forty-Niners and we had a rough game last night."

It wasn't even football season but she didn't have a clue.

"Hey, see that guy right over there?"

I was pointing at Chris, who was at the stage rail very happy that the magazines he kept hidden in his cell had come to life only a couple of feet from his face. I peeled a hundred bucks from a roll that was not nearly what it had been a week before.

"Why don't you take that guy to a private booth and make him feel special."

"I'd rather stay here and make *you* feel special."

"I admit I am much better looking, but you'll be surprised at what a gifted conversationalist he is."

She laughed, tossed her hair back, and I noticed that she had beautiful teeth; in fact, in the dim light of the bar she was very beautiful. What kind of twisted self-image or wounded past brought her here? You can never get the story without getting the backstory first. Some very religious men once brought a woman to Jesus. They said that she had been caught red-handed in an adulterous affair. The Mosaic Law prescribed the punishment as death by stoning. They wanted to catch Jesus in some kind of blasphemous act against the Jewish Commandments and so they asked Jesus:

"What do you say we should do with her?"

He bent down and began to write something in the sand, and one by one from the eldest to the youngest they disappeared. Jesus asked the woman:

"So where are your accusers?"

She said:

"I have none, my Lord."

He said:

"Neither do I accuse you. Go now and sin no more."

This is a very interesting statement given that he acknowledged that she was probably guilty when he said to go and sin no more, but he overlooked her sin when he said that he wouldn't accuse her. Sometime later Jesus was invited to dine at the house of another of these devout religious men, and a woman came who was not invited. This time I will quote verbatim from the scriptures in the book of Luke, chapter 7, verses 36–50:

One of the Pharisees asked him to eat with Him, and He went into the Pharisee's house and took His place at the table. And behold, a woman of the city, who was a sinner, when she learned that He was reclining at table in the Pharisee's house, brought an alabaster flask of ointment, and standing behind Him at His feet, weeping, she began to wet His feet with her tears and wiped them with the hair of her head and kissed His feet and anointed them with the ointment. Now when the Pharisee who had invited Him saw this, he said to himself:

"If this man were a prophet, he would have known who and what sort of woman this is who is touching him, for she is a sinner."

And Jesus answering said to him:

"Simon, I have something to say to you."

And he answered:

"Say it, Teacher."

"A certain moneylender had two debtors. One owed five hundred denarii, and the other fifty. When they could not pay, he cancelled the debt of both. Now which of them will love him more?"

Simon answered:

"The one, I suppose, for whom he cancelled the larger debt."

And He said to him:

"You have judged rightly."

Then turning toward the woman He said to Simon:

"Do you see this woman? I entered your house; you gave me no water for my feet, but she has wet my feet with her tears and wiped them with her hair. You gave me no kiss, but from the time I came in she has not ceased to kiss my feet. You did not anoint my head with oil, but she has anointed my feet with ointment. Therefore I tell you, her sins, which are many, are forgiven—for she loved much. But he who is forgiven little, loves little."

And He said to her:

"Your sins are forgiven."

Then those who were at table with Him began to say among themselves:

"Who is this, who even forgives sins?"

And He said to the woman:

"Your faith has saved you; go in peace."

You see, you can't know the story until you know the backstory and while scripture isn't definitive on this I would bet that these two women, were one and the same.

Jesus knew who she was and where she had been, and her act of gratitude and love was lost on the religious guy, but to Jesus it was the mark of the purity that now resided in her heart.

It is so true: He who has been forgiven much loves much.

So while I hate the entire production called the strip bar and everything it stands for, I can't judge the participants. I don't know the backstory. And as I looked at this beautiful girl not yet ravaged by the thief of life and the destroyer of dreams, I had to make a little comment to God.

"God, this sure looks like a rotten deal you gave us!"

Even as I said these words in my head I knew that God was grace and mercy and this world was a product of man's sin, not God's design.

Suddenly I thought of Leslie singing and playing guitar, and I thought of all those nights at Calvary Chapel, with my hands and my heart lifted up to God, and a voice said:

"Not for you, boy! This is the life you bought. You gotta finish paying the bill and you owe a lot."

"Well, then, I guess I better set up this hustle."

We spied out the office, the security—which was fat and weak looking—the entrances and exits, and we left confident that this was going to be like taking stuff from dead people.

We had five days to kill so we spent it getting seriously loaded and taking things, mainly drugs and money, from people who Billy thought should be relieved of the responsibility of having to care for them. He had quite a list of these folks and so the time flew by.

I also called Jerry in Hemet and told him that if all went well we would be delivering Storm and the girls within a couple of weeks. Three nights in a row we went up individually and cased the bar to see who closed up, and how long after the last customers left there would only be a minimal crew on the premises. We found that at least a couple of nights they had a little private party after closing, which was fine. There were four of us, we had the element of surprise, and I suspected that whoever was there was going to be fairly deeply involved in whatever pursuit had them going.

CHAPTER 8

I sat across the street, nose out of the alley, from the inferno listening to the approaching sirens and thinking about Chris. It went like this. Earlier in the day as we were planning this last little aspect of our deal we were sitting on the couch and I had volunteered to go light the match. We had really all gotten pretty close in the time leading up to the gig, rollin' around Sac and having our way. Chris was sitting next to me on the couch and I felt something drop into my lap.

"Figured you'd have room on that trailer for a little extra heading south."

It was the pink slip to Jack's bike. Signed, sealed, and delivered. It had been a really beautiful bike and I cursed my bad temper for what I did to it with that hammer.

"Cool, bro, and now I got the dough to fix it up again!"

We got to the bar's back service door about 2:45, after watching the comings and goings for a couple of hours.

Just the manager's car and one other car were in the lot. Chris got the door open lickety-split with some pretty fine picking skills and in we went. I had Bertha—my Ithaca Stagecoach twelve-gauge mag, sawed off to pistol size—Blue had a riot pump, and Billy and Chris both had .45 autos.

We padded our way quietly down the hall to the office and we could hear subdued music, talk, and some laughter. Pausing at the office door we grouped, looked each other in the eye, pulled up our bandanas, and snugged our ball caps down tight.

Billy counted down with his fingers, one-two-three, and the door came off the hinges...

Three guys hit the floor with a little assistance and were taped up so quick they didn't have time to register what was happening. On the desk were a couple of gym bags and four army-issue ammo boxes. I glanced at the booty on the desk and then took a closer look at the hostages. I recognized the bar's fat pervert of a manager, but I had never seen the other two guys before. There was a pendant hanging from one of the dudes' necks and the other had the same thing tattooed on his forearm. Club members, patch holders. A club I was familiar with, but strictly a local crew. Looked to me like their treasury was about to take a big hit and I tried to figure out how a small club had their fingers in such a big pie. I say big pie because Blue and Billy had all the bags and ammo boxes open and my heart was beating like a drum.

I had only seen that much money once before and that was when Blue and I had been tipped to a payroll robbery that yielded two hundred and seventy thousand dollars. The thing that really got my attention was the ammo boxes. They were full of some really white, really sparkly crank. We zipped up the bags and snapped shut the boxes, thanked the gentlemen who couldn't say "You're Welcome!" on account of the duct tape on their faces, and off we went.

The count said one hundred eighty thousand dollars and four pounds of very high-grade gak.

Forty-five grand and a pound of speed apiece.

I really had to wrestle with the whole arson thing after payday. I mean, we got the schwag, right? But I knew that Billy and Chris had given their word and even though we were all deeply deceptive and thrived on larceny, there was the matter of having to have an absolutely sterling character when it comes to integrity with certain things. I think my apprehension lay in the awareness that it had just all been so easy, not one hiccup, not one hitch. But then it had been that way with the payroll robbery Blue and I had done. We just walked in and picked up the money. I had gone to just pick up a couple of bags of dope and had more trouble many times.

So I sat there in the Ranchero watching the blaze, but I knew I had to go. And I knew if I got pulled over anywhere between here and the pad I was toast. I had spilled maybe less than a shot glass of gas on my pant leg, but it was enough to put me away for a very long time. Arson carries very heavy time because of the likelihood of death. I had gotten rid of all evidence, the gas can and so forth, and that in itself was accusatory. If I got pulled over and they asked me why I smelled I couldn't say I had run out of gas.

"See, here's my gas can, Officer."

Well, no matter what, smelling like accelerant and being in proximity to an arson was a surefire—ha-ha, surefire—ticket to the County Jail and more than likely a prison sentence that would be the last one. I pulled out on to Auburn Boulevard and headed home. About a half mile away I passed the cops and the fire trucks rushing to the scene. My heart did a little giddyup and since I was just about the only car on the road I really hoped the cop in the cruiser didn't wonder what my story was and decide to find out, or that later he would recall the Ranchero and start looking around for it.

The days and sometimes weeks following a caper were always anxiety riddled, and for me the consumption of opiates always increased and the speed tapered way down. Then suddenly and at no specific time the band around my chest would release and I could breathe.

For forty-five grand and a pound of crank it was worth it. I left the windows down on the Ranchero and went in the house, where I immediately stripped buck naked and threw all my clothes—tighty-whities, boots, and all—in the fireplace and turned on the gas. Later I would sift through the ashes and reburn any fragments and finally spread all of the ashes on the lawn in the backyard and water it profusely. I found Jack's hair trimmer, set it on number two, and buzzed my head, then threw all the hair in the fireplace as well. Finally I jumped in the shower with a scrub brush and scrubbed until I was a lobster.

I don't know what good all that would have done to battle the forensic sciences but it made me feel better, like I was being smart and thorough. I liked having a buzz, but man, I had some big ears. With the sudden hair loss they felt like they were flapping around. My watch read four fifteen and suddenly the weight of the day descended over me like a fog and I thought: *Maybe I should try a blast of that rocket fuel.*

Just then Blue's head popped up over the back of the couch where he had been crashed out.

"Nice haircut, Dumbo. You flyin' somewhere?"

"Oh, did I wake you up?"

"No, man, it was that hair trimmer that sounds like a lawn mower. Man, you and your anal retentive precautions! Oh, and stay out of the crank and go to sleep."

What was it with that guy? Steadily savin' me from myself. I threw on a pair of 501s and a T-shirt, stuffed my feet in a pair of Chuck's, stuffed a pistol in my waistband, and went to the door.

"You goin' to Stormy's?"

"Yeah, but I'll be on the couch."

"You forgot the marshmallows I got you, bro!"

Sure enough, on the counter was a bag of marshmallows and a coat hanger. We laughed and he sat up, his ghostly white spindly legs sticking out of his state issue–like white boxers. We were laughing hard.

"I wonder if a bag of marshmallows and a hanger could be construed as evidence?"

Chris and Billy emerged from the back room with Jack's old lady, and Blue and I just looked at each other and laughed harder. Blue shrugged his shoulders as if to say, *I can't call it man.*

Chris asked, "How'd it go?"

I looked at the dirty-legged girl and knew she knew. Sometimes gangsters were a tad bit overconfident in their hold on people, but what was I gonna do now? Kill the broad?

"Pretty sure by now it's a vacant lot. So as long as we're all here we might as well do a nightcap."

Chris went to the drawer that should have held cooking or eating utensils and came back with a brand-new ten pack of B-D U-100s, a glass of water, a Coke can, and a cotton ball. He threw ten balloons in the can, shot in five syringes of water, and cooked it all up. He made the girl draw hers up last.

"Second Thessalonians, chapter three, verse ten says: 'If anyone is not willing to work, let him not eat.' Or in this case, make them fix last."

I was flabbergasted. We had talked some, but this was a revelation and a testament to the potential of people to surprise and dismay. He just winked at me.

I had to crash. Things were getting surreal...

"See you guys tomorrow, really late."

They didn't ask me why I put my shoes on to walk fifteen feet. We all understood that in our life you don't go anywhere barefoot or unarmed. You might have to run down the street naked, but you will be wearing shoes and have a gun in your hand. I let myself in next door and peeked in at Ruthie and Margie, two beautiful little girls who stood a better than average chance of getting pregnant at fifteen and giving birth to drug-addicted babies. But for now they were innocent and to-tally unaware of the evil stench surrounding them. They were sleeping in a tangle of sisterhood, their blond hair intermingled and their arms around each other.

One of their pillows had been discarded on the floor and I scooped it up and headed for the couch. I passed Storm's door, which was open a few inches; there was a candle burning an invitation on the nightstand. Storm's long, honey-colored hair was fanned out on the bed and she looked lovely. I headed on to the couch. Life was already way too complicated. When I finally put my head on that pillow that smelled like Herbal Essence, my watch said five forty-five. The sleep of the dead descended quickly.

"Wake up, Uncle Eddie!"

This only preceded the assault of tiny knees and elbows by a matter of a second at best.

"Okay, I sent them…"

I reached in my pocket and slipped her a wake-up without the girls seeing. Then the babies scampered off to mischief land.

Eight o'clock…Two hours' sleep…Strangely I felt refreshed and alive. Having a big roll and a lot of dope will do that for ya. A dramatic contrast to those mornings when you wake up dope sick and there is nothing good in the immediate future. I don't live in fear of those mornings, but when they are upon me the fear is a stench sweat of dread and self-loathing. For the most part those wake-ups in hell only came when and if I was busted, which hadn't happened for a long time. I could smell coffee and I heard the sound of bacon hitting a hot pan, so I knew Storm had handled her morning business. The business of letting the devil hook up his puppet strings to the eyelets on your soul so he could have you dancing to his dark dirge all the live long day.

I thought about the run of prosperity we were presently enjoying and I wondered when it would all come crashing down. At any second the door could come crashing in, the result of some overlooked detail or the loose lips of someone who had won the confidence of Billy or Chris. I was always surprised at how people were so free with information that could cause them to break out in handcuffs. Giving potentially damaging information in exchange for a little recognition, a little hero worship.

I needed to get up and do a shot before I started getting freaky paranoid. We planned well, we executed flawlessly, and Billy and Chris were exemplary partners in larceny.

"Storm, where is your outfit? I gotta do my wake-up."

This chick was way out, man—she actually wore an apron in the kitchen. Used to tease her about it all the time, call her stuff like Dolly Madison, Betty Crocker, Chef Boyardee. She pulled a rig out of her apron pocket and flipped it to me.

"Don't bend up a good spoon, there's a cooker on the top of the medicine cabinet."

"You really think I'd take a spoon out of the drawer after the dressing down you gave me last time?"

"I'm glad you remembered; now hurry up, breakfast is almost ready."

"Yes, ma'am!"

I did my best little soldier impersonation and headed to the bathroom. I was thinking that this was as close to normal as it ever got for us. Storm still put two hot meals a day on the table and insisted that everyone be there to eat breakfast and dinner. She made peanut butter and banana sandwiches with the crust cut off, served with carrot and celery sticks and a glass of ice cold milk for lunch for the girls every day. Adult participation was optional but only at this one meal. If you were staying with her you better be at breakfast and dinner. I sat on the toilet with the bandana around my arm and the rig in my vein and was surprised by drops of water landing on my arm right where the needle was buried...Just as I was pushing the plunger home, I realized they were tears...

CHAPTER 9

We had the U-Haul packed, the three bikes loaded on the trailer; everything was gassed up and we were ready to go. The girls wanted to ride with Blue. That was prophetic. Still just little girls and already they wanted to be seen with the rough-cut biker and three Harleys rather than in a U-Haul with their mom.

"I don't know if You hear me, God, as far as I am from You, but if You do I just want to ask You to protect Margie and Ruthie from this world we are all subjecting them to."

A scripture came to mind, from Proverbs, chapter twenty-eight, verse nine:

"One who turns away his ear from hearing the law, even his prayer is an abomination."

I don't know, maybe He would make an exception since I was praying for a pair of innocent little girls.

All the dope and most of the cash were stashed in the nose of the truck, in front of all of Storm's household goods. We had kept out a grand and had picked up a paquete of smack downtown. We also kept out a couple of grams of go-fast to make the trip go fast, hardy har.

Storm sent the girls to play on the swing set in the backyard one last time and all the grown-ups filed into what had been Jack's pad and was now effectively crime central for Billy and Chris to do a good-bye, one-for-the-road fix. It was ten thirty in the morning and promising to be a hot day. Storm had always liked to lay out in the sun. She would get her folding chaise longue, a spray bottle of water, a big tumbler of iced tea, and just hang out in the yard in a bikini. She would always prop one of the stereo speakers up in the window and have the tunes cranked. Marshall Tucker was a fave.

This morning she was wearing a pair of cutoff jeans, a little big in the waist so she had to fold the waistband over and they rode right on her hips; a wife beater knotted at the very top of her midsection; and Chuck's with no socks. The morning sun was bathing her in its honey-colored light as she perched on the edge of the couch, tearing the filter off a red to use for a cotton. Iit illuminated the fine dusting of itsy-bitsy golden hairs that covered her belly and her thighs.

Suddenly I wanted to drive the Ranchero and have Blue drive with Storm. She hadn't been strung out long enough to have been ravaged by the drugs and she was still stunning in a young mom kind of way. The combination of her very pronounced mothering posture and the hint of the teenage girl, even though she was in her midtwenties, was extremely alluring. We had already opened the Pandora's box of romantic involvement but we had let it slide, and had been letting it slide for a while now. It was very hard because I knew I loved her desperately and I knew she loved me too, but Ricky had been gone less than four months and his shadow loomed large around his three girls.

In the brief time I had shared her bed, Ricky's bed, there were times when her gentle sobbing would wake me up and then she would take hold of me to ease her pain. I would let her but it was way too much for either of us, and then one day it was just over. One morning I just moved my stuff from her room to the hall closet next to the living room and started sleeping on the couch. She upped her heroin intake to compensate but there was very little I could do about that at the time. But now I had a hundred and fifty number-four codeines and about thirty Nembutals and when we got to Jerry's she was going to kick—or at least that was *my* plan.

"Earth to Eddie, come in, Eddie!"

"Wassup, Billy?"

"Man I thought you were gonna start drooling and you ain't even fixed yet, Dawg!"

"I was just…what did my granny call it? Oh yeah, wool gathering. Thinkin' about the road; leaving North Sac; you guys."

"Ha! That is funny because I woulda thought you were thinkin' about Storm, the way you were locked on her like a pit bull locks on a stray cat."

"Yeah, well, you see right through me, bro, but then what can say, I love her…" And I wanted to add, "And I just want to take her and make her mine and find a little house in the OC for her and Margie and Ruthie and me, and get a stinkin' job and quit killing myself with this stinkin' dope and be a family. BUT I CAN'T DO THAT NOW, CAN I, 'CUZ SHE

BELONGS TO A DEAD MAN AND HE WAS A GOOD MAN AND IT'S HIS FAMILY AND ALWAYS WILL BE, AIN'T THAT RIGHT, STORM?"

It got real quiet at that revelation, which was not what anybody expected me to say, least of all me. Storm was tied off and had the outfit clamped between her teeth as she slapped her arm to bring a vein up. She stopped set the rig down on the table and looked at me piercingly, I mean direct and deep.

"I love you too, Eddie, and you know it..."

It was the first time I had ever seen Billy or Chris uncomfortable and it made me laugh. Then we were all laughing.

"Shall we watch today's episode of *General Hospital* or *Ryan's Hope* before we get on the road?"

Blue chuckled at his own attempt at humor, but Storm was still looking at me and it looked like she was challenging me. Was she challenging me to step up and be and do all those things I had not said out loud? Well, we had a long drive ahead and now I knew who was driving what.

"Let's burn rubber!"

Nowadays that is a very common colloquialism, you hear it everywhere, all the time, but the very first time I had ever heard it said was when Storm said it.

We were all at a bar in Clanaheim, the Chez Paris, and it was getting tense. A little scuffle broke out and the bartender went for the phone, Storm said:

"Hey, guys, we better burn rubber..."

It was the most natural thing, just rollin' off her tongue, but I know for a fact she invented that saying—and I'll fight over it too!

Ricky's brother Warren came around the side of the house with the girls and helped get them loaded up, then there were hugs all around and we fired 'em and burned rubber!

Three days later Jack shot Chris in the head at a red light and got away, but not for long because within the week Billy had found him and pretty much dismembered him alive and dropped his pieces in Folsom Lake. They got Billy at a fancy hotel in North Lake Tahoe with all the speed and all the money and—get this—Jack's dirty-legged girlie. They tried to get Billy the death penalty for special circumstances, lying in wait, but after fighting his case from the county for six years he ended up with a life sentence. Blue and I sold our gak and spent our money frivolously and moved on to more capers. If I ever see Billy again all I will be able to say is: "You are one stand-up cat!"

CHAPTER 10

Margie and Ruthie were trying so hard to look cool in the hot-rod Ranchero with the bikes on the trailer behind. We had managed to fit the roll-away in the U-Haul on account of the third bike. Blue's bike looked as fine as ever, my shovel was still bruised up from the wreck, and Jack's bike looked hammered, literally. To me it kind of looked like a rolling junkyard and it made me a little sad, especially in light of the fact that I was going to have to follow it all the way to SoCal. On the other hand, I was in possession of a big wad of cash and enough speed to put both those bikes in show condition in no time.

I hopped up in the cab of the truck and Storm was hesitating on the passenger side, looking at me like she expected me to give her a leg up.

"Quit fooling around and just get in the truck!"

"Oh, okay, Sir Galahad…"

"Girl, I have seen you knock out full-grown men, so get in!"

I was thinking of the night when Blue and I first got to Sactown and we all went to a redneck bar called the Loading Chute. I don't remember how it all started but it ended up in a bucket of blood when fists no longer sufficed and it escalated to knives and pool cues. I had almost fallen down, slipping on what I thought was beer on the floor, but looking down I realized it was blood and my eyes followed the stream to under the pool table where the guy I had stabbed a few minutes before was lying, taking inventory of his condition. In the few seconds I had been distracted some cowboy had coldcocked me and as I was going down I saw Storm swing a pitcher in a big haymaker arc and knock that boy clean out. Straight-up sleepy time. She got me to my feet and we retreated out the door with Blue bringing up the rear. We blazed out of there in the Ranchero too outnumbered to continue, two bikers and one chick against a bar full of rednecks.

That was the night Storm and I began our brief romance.

I was jolted out of my reverie by first one long tan leg and then another sliding up next to me on the bench seat of the truck that suddenly seemed considerably narrower than it had a moment ago. Blue started out toward Madison Avenue, which would take us to the 80 freeway. I kerchunked the truck into gear and off we went.

Storm pulled a bandana out of her hip pocket and unrolled it to reveal a rig that was as full as it could be and still keep the plunger in.

"Speedball, just like I learned from you when you mickeyed me leavin' the old man's farm."

She slid over close and said:

"Gimme yer arm, Sport…"

She clamped her hand around my bicep and expertly found a vein. I watched my blood swirl up into the rig and she pushed the plunger, but only halfway, and then she pulled it out. As the mixture of high-power speed and 22 percent pure heroin threatened to saw me in half, exploding in two different directions seemingly separating me somewhere between my gut and my brain, I watched her as she found her sweet spot and again blood swirled up in the chamber.

She shoved that plunger home and as she pulled it out and threw the rig out the window she said:

"Now we are forever one, my love."

Chicken skin was rising up her arms and her belly and running all down her thighs. I outweighed her by at least eighty pounds and that jolt had hit me pretty hard.

"You okay, Storm?"

"I'm so fine, Eddie…Also…Oh Eddie, I gotta say this and I gotta say it right now: I love you, I have always loved you, that's why I cried after we…you know…I felt guilty because I had cheated with you in my mind for so long and when Ricky died the first thing I thought of was you. When Blue called and said he was coming he didn't say you were with him. The conversation was so short but when he showed up at the door and there you were standing all proud and beautiful behind him, my heart near exploded. And here we are in this truck headed for Hemet, both strung out to the caps and you thinkin' yer gonna drop me off at Jerry's and go gangstering with Blue. I'm confused, my love, but I've got your blood in me now and so you can never really leave me."

I said the only thing I could say:

"Shut up, woman, you are out of your mind."

But when I put my hand on her leg and smiled at her she jumped up in my lap and started kissing my neck. I looked ahead to the Ranchero and Margie and Ruthie had their faces pressed up against the glass of the rear window, and Blue was locked on to us in the side-view mirror.

That was a lot to digest on the heels of an earthquake of a hit, that's for sure.

The air was thick and suffocating in the cab of that truck even with the windows wide open. I had just noticed that the air conditioner was blowing hot, wet air that kind of smelled like dog and cigarettes. Storm started laughing in her high, sweet way—it came from her belly but somewhere between there and the atmosphere it was turned magically into one of those expressions of recklessness, expectancy, and joy. The kind of sound that gave birth to the saying, "Laughter is the best medicine."

She had seen my frustration but she knew she had the solution. She was carrying one of those woven Mexican Indian totes that always reminded me of Faith and of Hope as well, and of a time when innocence still had the greater hold on my life than the evil that consumed me now. So here is a snapshot of the kind of chick this was. She reached in the bag and pulled out one of her quart spray bottles. She misted me and immediately goose bumps came up and I was almost chilled. The cab was filled with the scent of jasmine and a whisper of patchouli. She had this little grin on her face that said, *Preeetty much perfect, ain't I?*

She had three more of those bottles in that bag.

Suddenly I was furious with God, with Ricky, with myself because I just clearly saw all of the little girl, of the mom, of the capacity for the greatest love; all the wit, the spontaneity, the passion for those around her; the caretaker, the solution finder, the peacemaker, the laughter bringer. And overlaying it all was a transparency and in that transparency was etched her portrait, a portrait of the future, and I knew I would have to see the transformation, the metamorphosis.

The transparency portrait was a sick and twisted picture of a woman worn and old, eaten alive as a leper by the devastating union of drugs and time, a woman devoid of hope, stripped of all of the vibrance that had once defined her. Her cheeks were hollow, her skin the gray shade of death, her smile deteriorated into a rictus of rotten teeth and pain. I recalled the things I had wanted to say after my confession of love at the communion table of addicts where we shared in the supper of Satan, eating his flesh and drinking his blood with the arrogance of the self obsessed rebelliousness of fools. I had thought:

And I just want to take her and make her mine and find a little house in the OC for her and Margie and Ruthie and me, and get a stinkin' job and quit killing myself with this stinkin' dope and be a family.

That was such a load of manure! It was just never gonna be like that; in fact, it wasn't going to get within a thousand miles of that zip code.

I had become convinced that change was impossible and this desire of mine, all noble and lofty, was the biggest fantasy of all in a life that was nothing but fantasy. People like us never changed, we just got slowly eaten alive, slaves to our own debauched appetites that ravaged us like leukemia. The difference was the cancer or the leukemia victim is innocent; we are as guilty as hell.

"Eddie, what's wrong?"

I looked over and all I saw was light and perfect beauty, but the true story was written in the darkening scar tissue of her forearms, where the toxic chemo therapy of our sin gained entrance and began its unholy mission to devour our souls.

"I'm cool, girl."

Under my breath I muttered:

"I don't know who I hate worse God, You or Satan…"

CHAPTER 11

By the time we got to the 99 I was completely road ready, sublimely speedballed, crackin' Juicy Fruit like a jackhammer, eatin' up the road with my frosted eyeballs way faster than it was going under the truck. Storm was drinking in the wind, hair blowing back, Wayfarers shading sparkling eyes, a half smile on her lips. I had to look away.

The road rhythm grabbed ahold of me and I started trippin' on the birth of this tribe of ours. Felony Flats, the Slater Slums, H.B., SoCal. All of us in our own orbit, a loose kind of dope and bike community. Snow Frog, Murdoch, Mikey Boy, Little John Curry, Chrissie, Ricky, and Storm—those were the main players—and me, Eddie. There was always a new injection of dirty-leg girls and bit players that would run for a while but then fade away. The sisters were Chrissie and Storm—they commanded respect and protection. Blue was still in prison and none of us knew him then, but when he showed up he became the catalyst. It was he who saved us—or at least saved me.

Me and Frog's pad was a condemned wood-frame, two-bedroom built in the twenties on an alley called A Street, right off the corner of Beach and Warner. It was abandoned so we tapped into the electrical and the water of the huge apartment complex next door and made it home. At first we thought for sure we'd be given the boot after a couple of weeks, a month at most, but after six months we were getting pretty comfortable. It was almost as if we were invisible.

Even the cops that drove by looked the other way, which was exceptionally hard to believe since, in a deep tweak after this enchantress named Robin had materialized from San Francisco with a product she called The Quicksilver, we had gotten extremely wired and spent two days painting the entire house, windows and all, flat black. We painted with brushes, obsessed, in the heat of the day with sweat sticking our shirts to our backs, and at night by the light of halogen lights powered by our pirated power from next door. It was as if we were invisible.

In fact it was so strange that as the months went by we became this little microcosm of puppets seemingly on the strings of a puppeteer, the mystical enchantress Robin. I began to suspect that we were in reality an elaborate experiment in sociology conducted by some university and that everyone—the police, the entire apartment complex next door and even a couple of the players—were in on the scam, particularly a cat named Perry. And at the helm of the entire twisted petri dish was Robin, this newcomer from faraway who somehow captured all of us with the Quicksilver wire.

It was a theory that was born in a nugget of plausibility. This cat Perry was in fact a sociology professor at UCI, and somehow he had met one of the crew at a bar on Beach Boulevard called Lucky John's Too. He had a pad right by me and Frog's shack and so a couple of the girls kind of moved in on him. We were all shooting a little heroin and doing club crank that was good because we got it before the cut got in it. Perry liked the speed and so since he had a paycheck and a pad he kind of got adopted.

One night we were all sitting around at Perry's, Frog, Ricky, and I baggin' up ounces and the girls all tweaking on playing a marathon session of backgammon. The backgammon thing had really taken hold, with the girls all getting their own boards and customizing the cases and doing scrimshaw on the pieces.

There was this one chick who wasn't really tribe but desperately wanted to be.

Her name was Monica and she was short, fat, and had really bad skin. She was just the kind of girl that my bro Moose went for and so she got to hang out. This chick could shoot a stinkin' tablespoon of gak in one shot. When she mixed up a hit it was so thick she could barely get blood to show in the syringe. She would do one of her gargantuan shots and sit down at the coffee table playing backgammon for three days. I never saw her eat and I marveled at her fatness.

So one day when everyone was finally sleeping, I was still up and I was patrolling the windows with Bertha, my sawed-off twelve-gauge mag, when I spied Monica's board on the table. I dunno what happened but I looked down at Bertha and kind of held it up with Monica's board case behind it, backdropping it, and it came to me that of all the cases the girls had been customizing hers was by far the coolest. It had a definite biker look. I had been looking for a case for Bertha and man, it looked like it would fit.

Before I knew it I had the guts ripped out of that case and had Bertha snuggled inside. I remembered there was some foam in the garage so I went and cut it to the shape of the "Gauge" and glued it in place.

"Voila!" Satisfied with my handiwork I got sleepy and went to lay down in one of the bedrooms with my new case on my chest. When everyone else began to wake up Monica went looking for her board and when she found it she was not pleased with what I had done. I knew this because all of her considerable weight was on my chest and she was beating me about the ears with the fated case, which was weighted by the couple of pounds of death merchant it was carrying.

I did the only thing I could do: I punched her right in the kisser. I thought she was behaving irrationally already, but now it escalated to outright insanity.

Her banshee wailing brought everyone into the room, with the hulking Moose last to arrive on the scene. Her nose had erupted in a fountain of blood and snot and she jumped for the door, screaming at the top of her lungs. When she got to the front door and flung it open, everyone was right behind her, but we all stopped short because in the open doorway was this chick who looked like Glinda, the good witch from *The Wizard of Oz*. She was carrying an old-fashioned carpetbag.

"Hi guys, I'm Robin. Perry said I could stay here for a while."

Then she did an almost imperceptible thing that I can only describe as a kind of shape-shifting or atmosphere-changing action. It was like everything froze for an instant and then again the door flew open and she was standing there and she said:

"Hi guys, I'm Robin. Perry said I could stay here for a while."

It was an instant rewind. We had no idea how long "a while" would turn out to be, or how many inexplicable things were going to happen in that time. Also I was dead certain she wasn't Robin. I had my doubts as to whether she was human or even real. But in that brief moment, that initial encounter, she saw me more than she saw anyone else. And as faded as His image may have been she saw Jesus in me and when she did she marked me as both an adversary and a challenge. Somehow way down deep inside of me I realized who, or I should say what, she was, and I knew things were about to get very spicy, *muy picante...*

There was an "I see you!" moment for both of us that rocked me back on my heels, and for the first time in a long time I felt fear. I had been lost for what seemed like a lifetime, lost in a spoon, lost in a tangle of the basest and most debauched aspects of my character—or lack of character—and in that moment of recognition I felt afraid. But mixed in was a sliver of hope, for if this apparition of Glinda the good witch, that sweet appearance masking a deep malevolence, and that dark being saw a light in me that was a potential threat, then maybe even though I was lost I was not forgotten.

"I love you, my child, and I will always be with you."

CHAPTER 12

When Robin walked through that front door the game changed; we all changed. She saw Monica's blown up and bloody schnoz and took her by the arm to the sink in the kitchen. On the way she set her carpetbag on the couch. She went to the second drawer of the kitchen cabinet where the clean dishtowels were and grabbed two. She didn't hunt for them, she went straight to the drawer. Chrissie told me later that it made her think she had been there before, but I knew better.

Expertly she whipped a barstool over in the front of the sink, turned on the water, blew over to the freezer, and filled one of the dishtowels with ice, all while depositing Monica's ample back patio on the stool. She held the other towel under the faucet and then began cleaning the blood and the boogers off of Monica's astounded face. When she finished her ministrations she shut off the water, wrung out the dishtowel, handed the ice pack to Monica, deftly hooked the barstool with her toe, sliding it back in place, and led Monica over to the couch, all with more economy of movement than I had ever seen. She sat down on the couch with Monica, her carpetbag between them.

This Robin had just won her first disciple. I could see it in Monica's eyes: *Someone cares.*

"Men can be such punks…"

She was looking right at me.

How did she know I was the one who fattened up Monica's pimply mug?

Then she said:

"Enough of that. Gather round, everyone, and let's look into something beautiful!"

Out of her carpetbag she pulled a jar—not a Baggie, not a film can, but a crystal jar with an ornately made sterling cap. It was about the size of a Smucker's family-size jam jar. What was in it was not powder but looked like windowpane acid, uniformly perfect little iridescent squares, luminous crystals, and when she held that jar up to the light coming through the window it was like a prism. It must have been close to a pound.

"This is The Quicksilver. Everybody get out your tools and let's begin this journey..."

In the pad that morning were, as you know, myself and Fat Monica (aka Schnoz), Frog, Moose, Chrissie, and John Curry. Perry was teaching sociology at U.C.I. wired on speed but it was funny with Perry: he never seemed high or tweaked out. And as it would turn out this Stevie Nicks doppelganger never seemed high, but I had watched both of them do hits big enough to drop an NFL lineman, or maybe two.

Everybody dispersed to retrieve their rigs and cookers, but when we all reassembled Robin had seven antique silver spoons set out neatly on the coffee table, each with identically bent handles so they sat perfectly level on the surface. She had a little bottle of water of the same vintage look as the glass jar and the spoons and it was getting very ceremonial. Dope fiends love ritual so everyone was deep in it. From somewhere she produced a little teeny spoon identical to the spoons on the table but much smaller. I would say it could hold a half teaspoon.

She dipped into her antique jam jar with her perfect little spoon and began to deposit the contents into presumably our spoons. She put maybe five or six of the perfect little squares in each antique silver spoon and when she did she started speaking.

"This is the Quicksilver Wire and it is absolutely one hundred percent pure and it is one hundred percent sacred. You may keep these spoons as gifts, and as I know you shoot heroin in those dirty little soot-stained cookers you must never taint your vessel with anything but the Quicksilver."

Moose was a big boy, probably 260 or so, and as she began to fill the spoon in front of him he said:

"I think I need more."

"You can think whatever you like, Richard, but let's try this first, okay?"

Smile from her so bright it would melt gold, and nobody but me noticed that she had used his name and they had never met. In fact I was sure I was the only one in that crew that knew his name because we had been busted together.

"Backgammon, I love backgammon!"

Suddenly that time-stop sensation came over the room again except she and I weren't in it, we were alone among the others. She looked at the backgammon board and my gaze followed hers. A white piece from the side of the board where she sat moved over to an unguarded black piece on the side where I sat and took it out, but no one had touched the board.

"Eddie, why can't you get your Panhead running?"

"What?"

"It's because you are slipping into this garbage crank that robs you of power, and you are so tweaked you didn't even notice you put hydraulic lifters in and are trying to adjust them like solids."

"What, so yer a wrench now?"

" I am many things, Young Edward."

Her voice was Hope's and Hope was the only person who ever called me Young Edward. And as I looked at her she became Hope, a woman I had desperately loved as a mentor, a mother, and the object of my adolescent idolatry and fantasy. She was also the one I had killed with the heroin that softened her grief at the loss of her husband, but also hardened her heart to stone until it crumbled and all that was left was the husk of a once magnificent woman. A toothless apparition of unholy inhumanity in the face of what at one time held a smile that lit my world on fire. Just as suddenly as it froze, time moved again.

I was reeling. It wasn't so much that I was in disbelief, I had grown up in the sixties and on a steady diet of every kind of psychedelic concoction—Purple Owsley, Lemon Sandoz, and hundreds of doses of Laguna's own Orange Sunshine. I had seen more than just a few supernatural events. Nothing will ever convince me that those events were mere hallucinations. The LSD opened up doors into a separate realm, a separate yet very real place, but it was a place that God had designed to be left alone. While the seekers of that place thought they were finding enlightenment, what was really happening is they were being seduced by what at first appeared to be a Utopian universe but in reality was a carefully concealed gateway to a place as far from God as far can be.

So the fact that I was reeling was not in disbelief of what I was seeing, it was in the realization that the Utopia Satan had cloaked his hell with in an endeavor to keep the truth hidden had been stripped away. What had been a quest for truth and love just ten years before had become degraded into a culture of hypes, liars, and thieves. The only love left was the love of the rush, the love of being as detached as possible from feeling what was real. Everything had become an acceptance of the counterfeit and a promotion of a life without truth. So I was reeling not in disbelief but in anticipation. I was looking forward to a dance with the devil, the contest that began at the doorway that had opened, revealing the spirit being Robin. I had no illusions now, this one was a manifestation of evil. This being may have been hiding in flesh and blood but a demon was in our midst. I suddenly felt more alive than I had in a long time. Oh, but I was so foolish!

I recalled a scripture I had read once when I had been living in truth, a long time ago and a lot of damage in the past. Yeah, there was nothing but scorched road and smoking wreckage in my rearview. The scripture was from the sixth chapter of the book of Ephesians and it went like this:

"For we do not wrestle against flesh and blood, but against principalities, against powers, against the rulers of the darkness of this age, against spiritual hosts of wickedness in the heavenly places."

What eluded me somewhat was the fact that as I proposed to wrestle darkness I myself was completely in darkness, devoid of any light whatsoever. There was no way I could prevail.

There was another scripture that I had read way back at Calvary with Craig and Leslie. It came from the book of Romans and it said this:

"Yet in all these things we are more than conquerors through Him who loved us For I am persuaded that neither death nor life, nor angels nor principalities nor powers, nor things present nor things to come, nor height nor depth, nor any other created thing, shall be able to separate us from the love of God which is in Christ Jesus our Lord."

For that to apply I had thought one must be actually in the Lord and I clearly was not so defeat was assured, but was it really? For here thirty years later I am the last one standing and I am writing a story about dead people. Yeah, I wasn't in the Lord but surely for the results to be what they are then He was certainly in me...

Let the wrestling begin...

"You don't need much water, Eddie, just a couple of drops."

I shrugged and squirted all but a teeny bit into the carpet. As I nosed my rig, carrying a lot less water than I had ever used to slam toward the spoon, that Quicksilver as she called it just sucked the water out viciously; it seemed as if I hadn't even pushed the plunger. In the spoon was a perfect pool of an oily yet crystal clear rainbow-edged liquid. I reached for a red from the pack on the table for cotton from the filter and Stevie, aka Glinda, aka Robin stopped me.

"You don't need that."

I drew up my hit sans cotton and what had been less than one unit of water had suddenly grown to almost four. The combined volume of water and product could have in no way equaled that amount; it had grown exponentially.

I drew up that hit knowing that the world was about to change dramatically and that when I pushed that plunger home I was maybe going to a place from which I would never emerge. Everyone else was deeply involved with their own ritual and Robin set her rig down on the edge of the backgammon board.

"Eddie, show me to the ladies room, would you please?"

I put my rig down opposite hers and stood up. She stood up as well and floated over, taking my arm like a countess taking the arm of her escort to make an entrance to a ball. I realized from her speech and her movements that she was deeply given to the theatrical. I rightly imagined that it was due to having been the center of attention in any group for quite some time. She had the air of a monarch, the aura of a queen. Outwardly she was all smiles and grace but hidden just below a thin veneer was a powerful predatory force. She came bearing what she presented as gifts, but I imagined the truth in her. She was there to suck the blood of those she would soon make her minions.

She was a vampire who fed on the weakness of those who became caught in her web of hedonistic hungers. She was the new face of the same old demon who came in the sixties in a disguise of love, peace, and LSD. The costume had changed but the heartbeat that drove the creature was the same old heart of Satan. She had singled me out, oblivious to the others except for a cursory and superficial communication. For her purposes at this point they were inconsequential. I was the object of all her attention and I knew exactly why.

"Wait for me here Eddie."

She went in and closed the door. After a moment I heard her singing.

"In the day we sweat it out on the streets of a runaway American dream
At night we ride through mansions of glory in suicide machines
Sprung from cages on Highway 9,

Chrome-wheeled, fuel-injected
And steppin' out over the line
Baby this town rips the bones from your back
It's a death trap, it's a suicide rap
We gotta get out while were young
`Cause tramps like us, baby we were born to run."

That song was my mantra, I listened to it fifty times a day. Yeah, she knew secret things but why did she feel this need to impress me? Was it supposed to be intimidation? I suspected so—or no, maybe she was issuing a challenge. Surely she knew I recognized her, we'd had that moment at the threshold of the door. I thought about the way she looked at everyone in a dismissive way—not condescendingly or openly, but veiled. And then she saw me and it was as if she had acquired her target. She emerged from the head wearing a saccharine smile, still humming the melody.

She sang sweetly, I will give her that.

"Tramps like us, baby we were born to run. Are you ready to run, Eddie, or are you just gonna keep standing still in this dung heap?"

We made our way back to the living room coffee table and resumed our positions. She reached down and grabbed both rigs and handed me mine.

Then Robin caught my eye and I have never seen such a hunger. She was hungry for what was left of my soul, she was voraciously hungry. Her eyes were screaming: *Do it, do it!*

I never pushed a load in that hard or that fast in my life, and as I pulled the needle out of my arm and the blood trickled down the inside of my elbow it hit me. When it hit me every piece on the backgammon board began to swirl and dance. No one saw it but me and Robin.

CHAPTER 13

"Eddie, if I can't change you I'm going to have to hate you."

We were in Perry's room. There were candles lit everywhere and I was flat on my back on the bed with my shirt off. She was straddling me and she was lovely…But my flesh recoiled at the realization of where we were. I wasn't even surprised or in wonder about how we got there. No, I recoiled at the intimate closeness I was having with a dead person. I recoiled because I already knew she was cold, cruel, and filled with a wicked spirit. Briefly I wondered how she got this way. What had happened to her? She looked about twenty-five and without discernible physical flaw. What was it that had taken over her life and what was the path it took to gain entrance? What had hurt her so deeply that she had given up on goodness, given up on life? Our tribe, our crew strung out to the bone, every last one of us, but none had given themselves over willingly to Satan. I knew that was exactly what Robin had done. She had signed a contract, entered into a dark covenant. What had been promised to her—riches, power, beauty? After Jesus was baptized by John, the Spirit of God took Him to the wilderness and after forty days of no food or water Satan met Him there at what should have been His weakest point. As Matthew described it:

Then Jesus was led up by the Spirit into the wilderness to be tempted by the devil. And when He had fasted forty days and forty nights, afterward He was hungry. Now when the tempter came to Him, he said, "If You are the Son of God, command that these stones become bread."

But He answered and said, "It is written, 'Man shall not live by bread alone, but by every word that proceeds from the mouth of God.'"

Then the devil took Him up into the holy city, set Him on the pinnacle of the temple, and said to Him, "If You are the Son of God, throw Yourself down. For it is written: 'He shall give His angels charge over you,' and, 'In their hands they shall bear you up, Lest you dash your foot against a stone.'"

Jesus said to him, "It is written again, 'You shall not tempt the Lord your God.'"

Again, the devil took Him up on an exceedingly high mountain, and showed Him all the kingdoms of the world and their glory. And he said to Him, "All these things I will give You if You will fall down and worship me."

Then Jesus said to him, "Away with you, Satan! For it is written, 'You shall worship the Lord your God, and Him only you shall serve.'"

Then the devil left Him, and behold, angels came and ministered to Him.

What had been Robin's weakest point wherein Satan came and made his offers, whispered his promises? Was it in the dark hole where she lay following a betrayal of trust by a strong man who had left her broken and battered in secret places? Was it in that hate-filled moment of realizing her own vulnerability that the tempter came and offered her a power sufficient to not only protect her but to exact a sweet revenge on any and all who fit, bore a resemblance to the description of her trust betraying assailant? How old had she been? Ten, twelve, fourteen?

I looked up and I searched her eyes and there was not one shred of that little girl in her anywhere. Her hands were in her lap and in them she held two identical little bottles. One of them I was sure was the bottle that held the water we all drew from to fill our rigs; the other was a mystery. She was just gazing at me curiously, waiting, I supposed, to see what I was going to do but I had the sensation of being an antelope just taken down by a lioness, waiting for the bite to the neck that would crush my spine and snuff out the light. She was lovely...

"You see, Eddie, we have a situation."

I was trying to remember that hit, the rush, but it was a blank. I did remember the moving of the backgammon pieces and I remembered that no one else saw it except me and Robin, a secret communication. I remember she had drawn up a dose herself and we slammed together and suddenly I realized that the trip to the bathroom had been a decoy. She had dosed me with something. It was very quiet in the house. The usual undercurrent of hushed conversation, the sounds of plumbing, chair legs scraping the floor, music, they were all absent.

"Where is everyone?"

"On little errands to start the ball rolling. Or, I should say, to start the Quicksilver train barreling down the track...Woot, woot!"

She was laughing a little.

"I wanted some time with you to iron out a couple of things."

"What things?"

I was about to ask her exactly how we got in here when she seemingly knew we were coming to that line of inquiry. She held up the two little bottles and gestured with the one in her left hand.

"Water."

She gestured with the one in her right hand.

"Not water, but rather Eddie's special little potion."

"So you slipped me a mickey, cleared out the house, lit a room full of candles, and got us both in here in a room full of props. What the hell for?"

"There is too much God in you, Eddie—He's dim, but He's there. And Eddie, there is no room for God in this little project we are about to undertake here in your beloved Orange County—at least not your God. There need to be some changes made in you, Eddie, so let me ask you: Do you want to ride? I mean, do you want to really ride like when you first got out of jail and ran away from those pretentious Christian idiots and their silly dogma and found your home place? You blasted those canyons like a stallion, Eddie. By the way, you should have bedded that girl,—what was her name, Amber, wasn't it? You know what happened to her, Eddie? Maybe I'll let you watch the tape sometime. Oh and what is it with you and sex, Eddie? Are you a eunuch?"

"Sex without love is no better than blasting off with a good speedball, so dope is my sex. Look around here, do you see any love? Do you see any candidates for love? Where am I supposed to find love? I'm a junkie."

"My oh my, Eddie, aren't you the provincial one."

"So cut to the chase, girl, my legs are fallin' asleep. What do you want me to do, sell my soul to the devil or some crap like that?"

"Yes, exactly that, Young Edward. Ha-ha, 'Young Edward.' Wasn't that what she called you? Her little pet name for the little pet that bit her, the little lap dog that killed her? Oh and wasn't Hope a beauty before you got her hooked? How do you live with that one, Eddie? Such a shame, but yes, exactly that, Eddddddiiiieeee. But for now I would settle for you just casting out the crucifix rider, the cross jockey, the perfect sacrifice, the sinless wonder. Just tell Him you no longer want His services, serve Him an eviction notice effective pronto, right now."

Those words cut me in a very deep, already existing wound that was festered and infected, then scarred over, but never healed. I wasn't going to let her know that.

"I don't know what you gave me but it seems to have not been the Quicksilver you have been bragging up, so how about we try a taste of that and then we'll continue this conversation."

I rolled her perfection off of me, picked up her carpetbag from the dresser, and chucked it at her. It hit her in the place she appeared most perfect. Good, didn't want to see anymore of that anyway. Suddenly Stormy appeared in my mind, and just as she did, Robin laughed.

"What was it you said, Eddie, 'No love, no sex'? I think Ricky will die young, so maybe there is hope that someday you will get a little. Okay, Sport, let's fix."

She reached into the large carpetbag and retrieved a small drawstring sack full of brand-new syringes. She also pulled out the jam jar full of her product.

In the bag with the rigs were a couple of those antique spoons and she set one of them on the bedspread. Out of the jar of product she pinched a little bit of the glass between her fingers and deposited it in the spoon, then she dipped her finger in her water bottle and flicked a few drops into the spoon with the crystals. They disappeared instantly, not even requiring a mix with the cap end of a rig. She drew it up and it almost filled the U-100. Again I was amazed at how much it increased in volume. She squirted half back and gave me the rig and then she drew up her half.

I had a bandana in my back pocket and I whipped it around my forearm as she put her arm across her thigh and then crossed her other leg over the top.

"Together, my friend?"

"Sure, let the good times roll…"

"*Mazel tov*, then."

I was watching the blood swirl up into her rig, I don't know, half expecting it to be black maybe, and she was intent on mine. We both began to push, our eyes locked into each other's like fighters at the weigh-in before the fight, attempting to raise ourselves up to a larger-than-life stature of intimidation and measuring each other at the same time. She was very beautiful so there was a disarming effect in her gaze, and when she sensed that I was feeling it her eyes lit up with that recognition. Oh, but the devil always tips his hand, shows his cards, because if she had masked that recognition of my weakness I might have fallen. But because she saw me and let me know, just in that slight change in her countenance, I was warned and in that warning was my salvation. At least for that moment.

I slammed the plunger home. It started in the center of my chest radiating outward, to my groin to the top of my head. It pushed the air out of my lungs as if I had been squeezed in a giant fist, and in fact I was because something had just gotten a hold of me that desired to never let me go. Suddenly I had the sensation of falling and with it came a vision. I was falling from the sky with thousands of others and as they fell they were being changed from beings of light and beauty into grotesque beings with cores of unadulterated hate.

How you are fallen from heaven, O Lucifer, son of the morning!

Just as quickly as it came it went and there was a dawning. The room became a very sparkly place, every surface giving off light, but I knew that the heart and soul of that light was a darkness so black that it had substance, it was impenetrable and its reality was the antithesis of light. It was evil of the purest form disguised as diamonds, posing as a treasure, but it was in truth absolute bankruptcy of the soul, and a bankrupt soul is a dead soul.

"Where are you, God? You said You'd always be with me. I thought You'd never leave."

But the truth was it was me who left, fell yet again to the seduction of the lie.

The grin on Robin's face really said it all. She knew as did all of heaven and hell that I was a just a punk in a tattoo suit. Just as weak as the runt of the litter.

CHAPTER 14

Frog and I had the Black House, as it came to be known. When it was built it was probably a beautiful little house, craftsman style set back from the street on the lot with a covered front porch and twin gables, giving the impression of a two-story. It was actually small, cottage-like, with two bedrooms and one bath.

We had made some modifications. The steps leading up onto the porch and the front door had become a ramp and the front door removed, the opening widened to make room for ape hangers. There was a heavy fabric veil serving as a door but riding up the ramp and into the house the veil would part cleanly in the middle and in we would ride. Every wall of separation had been torn down in the house except the bedrooms and the bath. It was just one big room and so we would blast up the ramp, get a little air going through the front door, slam on the brakes on the hardwood floor in the living area, and brodie to a stop, hoping to stop facing out the door.

Frog was a funny guy so he thought it would be cute to make a little puddle of oil right at the braking place. The couch was up against the farthest wall, which was where he posted up when he heard me coming down the street. We had a pit bull named Thor and a Great Dane named Loki who were on the couch with Frog. We also had some other pets that I will introduce in a moment. So I came flying up the ramp, got my front wheel off the ground going through the veil, and then everything went super slo-mo. I saw Frog and the mutts watching with malevolent glee. Yes, even the dogs were up for this sadistic little display.

I saw the oil and I knew right then what was happening, but I was powerless to change anything. Looking back I see that was a common thing in my life. So with perfect choreographed precision I laid the bike down and slid across the twenty feet separating me from where our other pets lived.

Our other pets lived in a stack of glass terrariums on the far wall of the kitchen. There were two reticulated pythons about eight feet each, three Western diamondback rattlesnakes, fat and sassy at six feet long, and some smaller domiciles housing about fifty scorpions and as many black widow spiders. When I say scorpions and black widows you need to understand that we fed them ten times more food than they would have ever gotten on their own. The abdomens on these black widows were as plump and rotund as overripe giant grapes. The crimson hourglass on their bellies shimmered bright against the raven's wing glossy blackness of their bodies. The rattlers were intimidating and the scorpions were as well, but those arachnids held in their purposeful movements a primal terror for me.

They were the object and cause of near hysteria in my heart and soul as I slow-mo slid across the floor, headed for a collision with a wall of poison and death.

I remember thinking, *Why do we have those again? Oh, that's right, because we are badasses!* A cacophony of breaking glass, hissing and rattling crescendoed through my skull as I jumped up like a jackrabbit and screamed like a twelve-year-old girl. A true badass for sure! Frog was quick, I'll give him that—he had those dogs out on the porch lickety-split and I was hot on their heels.

"What the hell was that?" I followed that question with a right cross to Frog's jaw. He grabbed my vest, fell backward over Loki, and all of us tumbled down the ramp and into the yard. We broke into the wild, cackling laughter of the deeply disturbed.

"We better try to do a round up."

I held out my hand and Frog grabbed it brother-style and I yanked him to his feet. First we put the dogs in the backyard and then we ascended the ramp and went to look in the front window, which was painted black except for a couple still-clear spots left unpainted for obvious reasons. It was late morning and the sun was shooting shafts of bright light through the unpainted back windows and the open back door (so much for the dogs being safe), and those shafts of light held in their brightness a most curious sight.

Robin was standing barefoot and completely naked in the center of the wreckage. She had the most magnificent hair, the color of tupelo honey and impossibly curly, hanging to the small of her back, and from there to the floor was pure loveliness and that pure loveliness was being ascended by a number of scorpions and widows. Seemingly unconcerned she was gingerly placing a totally docile six-foot rattler in a pillowcase. That serpent's body was fully twice as big around as her arm.

At the crown of her head was probably the biggest scorpion of the bunch and it was standing upright with its claws executing some kind of macabre salute. These reptiles should have been in a state of high agitation but they seemed almost entranced. I saw her face and her eyes were closed and she was singing. It was by far the strangest thing I had ever seen, but it was by no means half as strange as the things I was going to see.

She got all the snakes in their bags and we all piled in the cooperatively owned '69 Chevy Wagon, painted flat black with a big red skull on either side, and we went and bought a dozen flea bombs. I pretended to be sorry about the murder of our bug collection. So what were we doing with all these venomous critters living in the pad? We milked those rattlers and everyone knew it so the word venom got to be a kind of threat, challenge, and mystery all in one. Nobody ever wanted to fix at our house and it created such a mystique around Frog and myself. There were rumors galore but my favorite was that Frog and I had been giving ourselves injections of venom and gradually we became immune, but the side effect was that we had developed special powers. The speculation on what these powers were was wide and varied but we relished the notoriety.

I was in the backseat next to a couple of sacks of snakes and I had Robin's beautiful face right in the rearview from my vantage point.

"Robin's moving in with us, bro…"

She looked at me in that mirror and gave me the smile of the teenage girl, the crown going on her head and she is made homecoming queen.

"Of course she is…"

After a few weeks most of the scorps and widows had died from the massive bombing we did, but every couple of days you'd see one limping across the floor or dropping off a window ledge. I would have been worried about waking up with one or the other in my bed except that nobody slept. I had long ago gotten used to four and five days tweaking around, and if I lasted to six I would be seeing aliens posing as FBI agents posing as gardeners next door. If I made it to seven they were in the plumbing and the wiring, monitoring everything. It got to be sport, really, except for the fact that some of the hallucinations and imagined scenarios were absolutely real, as you will soon see.

Or maybe you won't, it depends upon your position on the super-natural.

Anyway, I was working on about eight days awake when Moose brought Coyote to the Black House. Now everyone in the tribe was pedigree Orange County, historic homies. OC bred, except Moose. Moose was from Mojave. He used to say:

"Where I'm from there is no town, nothing but desert, and it is so loose you could drag a dead body around behind your bike for a week and nobody would notice."

Moose was an enigma. The more speed he did the bigger he got and he tipped the scales at around two fifty. He was six-nine and had enough thick curly hair to stuff a mattress. His beard would get caught on his belt buckle when he stood up so every time he stood up he'd wince. I'd say, "Bro, just trim off two inches and voila, problem solved."

Moose always collected the most interesting girls, like his present flame fat Monica. He drove a 1971 Pontiac Catalina, satin black with black wheels and limo tint before satin black was the latest fad. It was very fast and very gangsta. I never saw Moose with a bike but one time he sat on mine and the image was comical. He made my '54 Pan look like a kiddie bike. Moose and I did a lot of crime together—we robbed connections mainly, but we'd do collections or hired mayhem. Once we took off a guy out in Desert Hot Springs for ten thousand Dilaudids and left the guy taped up on a chair in his living room. I remember saying:

"His old lady will be home by the time we get to Quartsite." (We were taking the product to Phoenix.)

Three days later we were on our way back and Moose said:

"I wonder if dude has re-upped? He would never expect a repeat."

"We can check it out."

The guy had a long dirt driveway leading to his hacienda-style desert house and we pulled in about nine thirty at night. All the lights were off and the place looked deserted, so since we were not above a burglary we went in. The house smelled like the dysentery ward in a T.J. hospital, oh so bad! Moose clicked on his mini-Maglight and the first thing we see are the biggest, roundest, most horrified eyes I have ever seen and that was the source of the smell. He was still duct-taped to the chair, and he was almost dead. He looked really confused like, *Am I about to get rescued or killed?*

His bare feet and hands were swollen and purple, and he was in a puddle of stench. I unsheathed my Schrade and cut him loose. I let him tear off his own face tape.

"You just sit tight, don't get freaky on us."

"Are you kidding me, man? I can't even stand up!"

Moose made a pot of coffee and some sandwiches, and I helped the guy get into the shower and get some clean clothes on. When we sat down at the kitchen table, the color beginning to return to normal on his appendages, Moose said:

"Man, we didn't want to kill ya, we thought for sure yer old lady would be home before long."

I think Moose and I were both a little shook up at how close we had come to murder one and kidnap.

Ron (we now were all on a first name basis) said:

"See the note on the fridge?"

I got up grabbed it and read this:

Ron, you are a selfish and rotten bastard, I'm out. I hope your life sucks! No longer yours, Crystal.

"Look, I am in a grip of pain. Would you go in my room and get my stash of pills for me, please?"

"Wanna do some chiva instead?"

"Never have..."

"Oh, well. Hey, man, the least we can do is pop your cherry!"

"Okay, why not at this point."

We fixed up a group cook in a huge spoon from his kitchen silverware drawer and we gave him his first shot ever of heroin.

Now you have to understand that a dope fiend rarely gets to see a person lose their virginity, so to speak, and it is quite a novelty.

Moose and I both had our chairs pulled up close to Ron and were almost sniffing him as Moose pushed that plunger to take him on the huge ride, the one time and one time only ride, because no matter how good it is it will never be like the very first time.

I watched him get a quick hitch in his breathing, the kind you get when you are surprised. It was that sudden split-second pause between inhale and exhale, the breath caught at the top of the inhale, and then came this slow heavy sigh of death. Not your death…well maybe not, but rather the death of every single thing that ever mattered. Every single thought or concern, fear or anxiety, resentment or sorrow is suddenly vaporized and all there is is sublime and perfect peace. Your body feels a way it has never ever felt in your entire life. It overshadows and dwarfs any sensation you have ever felt; even the passion and release of your deepest, most intense love affair is insignificant in comparison.

Ron looked at me and I watched his pupils shrink to pinpoints. Very quietly he simply said:

"Oh…"

So we killed him, after all. He just wasn't dead yet.

"Look, Ron, this is the strangest thing I have ever had happen to me."

Moose laughed kind of nervously. "You ain't kiddin'!"

"What did you pay for those pills?"

"You mean what do I owe for those pills? I haven't even paid yet, supposed to pay tomorrow."

"How much?"

"Forty thou…"

"I'll be right back."

I went out to the Pontiac and grabbed an ammo box that was holding the hundred thousand we got for ten thousand pills. I set the ammo box on the table and I knew that Moose was on the same page with me. I don't call it karma anymore but I did then. I counted out forty and put it in front of Ron, then made three stacks of twenty, one in front of each of us. Each man nodded approval at my proposition and then we just sat back, looking at each other marinating in the strangeness of this entire debacle.

"So, Ron, how's it lookin' down the road?"

"It looks just fine to me, man…"

We ended up doing a lot of business with Ronnie and amazingly he never once acted like he held even a whisper of resentment. I asked him once:

"What the heck man? Weren't you pissed?"

He laughed and said:

"Eddie, that was the most intense and exciting thing that ever happened to me. I had never felt that alive, man! After you guys left the second time I laughed my butt off for a half an hour and then I just sat on my couch and savored the heroin and the whole insane thing I went through taped to that chair. During that time, not knowing if I was going to live or die, somehow my hearing got hypersensitive. I swear I could hear stuff crawling around on the ground outside so I heard you guys as soon as you turned off the highway, and I recognized the sound of that car and I was not scared. Somehow I knew it was gonna be cool and the irony of the entire deal was hysterical. I had to fight to keep from laughing when you guys walked in. You should have seen your faces—man, it was priceless. Anyway, what I am trying to say is it was the most fun I've ever had!"

"Man, you are one crazy, freaked-out cat!"

Ronnie lived in the cell next to me on the ground floor of J Wing in Tracy for two years and I will say he was one stand-up bro.

We hopped in that bad-to-the-bone Pontiac and slung some gravel getting out of there. But my whole story was really about Moose's romances. We were heading back down Indian Avenue in North Garnett to get to the 10 Freeway and we stopped at the Speedy Mart to get some victuals and some gas, and there was a duffel bag leaning up against the wall. Next to it and the same height as it was this little girl. At least I thought it was a little girl, but it was not. It was Miranda, a twenty-year-old midget with nowhere to go. I couldn't help myself.

"What, did you run away from the circus?"

"Very funny, genius. Who's the Paul Bunyan guy with you?"

It was then that I noticed that she was really pretty and it was also just then that Moose walked up and I could tell by the look in his eye that it was on like Donkey Kong.

Yeah, Moose was a picture...RIP.

Like I was saying, I was working on about eight days awake when Moose brought Coyote to the Black House. He was very small and the first word that came to my mind was Cobra. He stuck his hand out to shake and it was as cold as ice. He was very tight looking, whipcord lean and muscular, about five-eight. His hair was jet black and braided in two pigtails that came to his belt. He had one of those beards that looked like it was the same kind of hair he had on his head. It was perfectly straight and perfectly groomed. In fact, everything about this guy was clean and polished. No fade on his 501s, his Logger boots were worn but boot blacked recently, and he was wearing a denim shirt that looked tailored. The thing was it all fit, homie looked real sharp. Hanging from his belt was a Rigid Bowie with a ten-inch blade. It was a knife I had coveted for quite a while.

"Eddie, this is Coyote. We've been pards for a long time so I can vouch, he wants an ounce of the Quicksilver. If that goes well he'll be good for a quarter pound a week."

Moose was given to cowboy colloquialisms like that. Like really, who says, "We're pards"?

"Come on in."

I was working on my Pan head in the living room and the dude walked around it nodding with approval. I said:

"I won't have that much here until tonight, but we have a little taste if you want to indulge. We can hook up later for the weight."

"That would be fine. I'd like to show you the stuff I build. Maybe you can drop off the QT at my pad and you can see what I'm working on."

We all did a shot and Coyote gave me directions. I agreed to be there around five thirty. The fact was I had at least a pound right there but who needed to know that, right?

At five forty-five I pulled my Packard into the driveway of the quint-essential biker compound: eight-foot cyclone fence, three big Dobies, a huge garage with commercial roll-up doors, and no windows on the front of the house. It would have looked like a prison yard except for the trees. Pepper trees with their boughs drooping gracefully like weeping dancers covered the property, providing a beautiful dappled light over the whole place.

Coyote spoke some German to his dogs and waved me into the garage.

We did the transaction and then he showed me a couple of bikes he was working on. He was a perfectionist and a very talented artist.

"I moved out here from Phoenix and bought this place last year. Too stinkin' hot in Arizona for me anymore."

Then *she* walked in. Or I should say she glided in on the breath of an angel.

Hair blacker than a raven's wing. Native American? Asian? Latina? I couldn't be sure, but she defied gravity when she walked. She looked at me quickly and when I saw her eyes my breath got caught in my throat. They were the color of emeralds.

"Sunshine! Get back in the house! I'm doing business."

"I'm sorry, Gator's on the phone and he's at the corner in the phone booth at the Chevron. He wants to come over."

"Just tell him to come over and don't come out here again."

As she turned and walked by me I caught the fragrance of some tropical flower—but I also saw the bruises on her upper arm and her neck and suddenly I wasn't gonna be friends with this punk. I recognized the sound of Gator's bike coming down the street. He was running upsweep fishtails and they have a very different and distinctive sound. I had known Gator for a long time. He was born and bred. He came through the gate and again Coyote spoke some German and the dogs relaxed.

"Hey, Eddie, how ya doin'?"

"Good, bro."

Gator pulled some cash out and laid it on the workbench.

"We're square. Is there any more product available?"

"Yeah, sure…Hey, Gator, when you were here the other day did you see an S&S Super B carb on the bench right here?"

"Nah, man, I sure didn't."

"Okay, cool, maybe it's in that box up there on the top shelf. Yer tall—would you reach up there and grab it down for me?"

"Sure thing, bro."

As Gator reached up with his right hand to grab the box he put his left hand on the bench to boost himself up a bit, and faster than I have ever seen anything that Rigid Bowie with that ten-inch blade took three fingers clean off that left hand. For a second it was dead silent and time froze, not even any blood. I could see the end of the bones, the veins, the tissue, everything, and then it was a cacophony: gushing blood like a garden hose on full blast, piercing screams, barking dogs, mayhem at warp speed. Except Coyote—he was just in slow motion as he casually scooped up Gator's severed digits and threw them one at a time to his dogs. I could hear their jaws snap shut as they snatched those fingers from the air. With more power than I would have thought he had, Coyote turned and slapped the screaming Gator.

"Shut up and get your thieving carcass off my property."

Gator looked at me but he was in too much shock to say anything. He ripped the bandana from his head and tried to stanch the flow of blood from his hand as he walked out to his bike. We both knew that I wouldn't get involved at that time. Even if I jumped in and made a stand it wouldn't get Gator's fingers out of the dog's bellies. There was going to be payback for sure but it was better that I didn't show my anger for what happened at the present. I got ready to duck in case Gator had a piece on his bike but it looked like he didn't because he sat on his bike, tied his bandana as best he could around his hand, and went about the painful business of getting his bike started. It took him three tries to get his bike moving because he couldn't pull in the clutch, but finally he lurched off down the street.

"I won't tolerate a thief of any kind."

I had never heard of Gator being anything but stand up and I knew he didn't need some lame S&S carb, so I didn't know what that was all about but decided to play uninterested for the moment. Coyote didn't know how well I knew Gator and the thing I found interesting was that he was so consumed with his own sense of self-importance that it didn't occur to him that two bikers from the same area might actually be good friends.

But in my mind a plan began to develop, out of which Gator would get revenge and some do-re-mi and I would get Sunshine. There was a lot to think about but whatever was going to happen this guy was about to get blindsided with a heavy dose of OC justice. I wondered what he would have done if he knew right then that I was gonna steal his bruised but beautiful woman. I was like a kid who passed by a shop window and caught a glimpse of the bicycle he had been dreaming about all his life. This was the first time since Michelle at Wonderland Avenue School, my beautiful scar-faced girl with whom I had been hit so hard with the hammer of love. Man, that was the sixth grade. Even so, that love was as real and pure as a newborn colt on wobbling legs stretching its neck for the sweetness of its mother's milk. It was a powerful hunger.

I knew absolutely nothing about this girl and she had come barging into my brain with the force of a locomotive and left me gasping for breath. It had all of the elements of a fairy-tale romance. She was stunningly beautiful and in trouble, held captive in the tower of the fire-breathing dragon and I was the lovelorn heroic knight who pined for true love and had never found it. So there it was...It just barreled into my brain like a herd of elk in the rut, stampeding the fences of logic and common sense and leaving them trailing behind the herd like the tin-can tail on the wedding car.

"Yep, you gotta steal the girl, she needs you to rescue her. She has to be his prisoner, she is too lovely to be with this little Hitler willingly."

This man was both little and he was small—little in stature and small in character. In the face of it I fancied him a coward as well. A man who only moved when the results were certain.

The things about Coyote that I had initially admired came out of the fog and laid naked their truth. They were nothing but carefully constructed props and he was the director of a play in which the protagonist had all the trappings of the real thing outwardly, but in reality the trappings were all he had: the lusciously beautiful and unattainable woman; the immaculately cultivated appearance; the highly pedigreed German dogs; the tastefully restored yet fully custom jet-black '67 Camaro. Then there was the state-of-the-art, ten-inch Rigid de-digitizer. Everything about him screamed: *"Look at me! I am the real deal!"*

Only the real deal doesn't need to announce itself.

The real deal doesn't parade itself, it just is.

It doesn't trumpet a fanfare when it arrives, at some point you just realize that it's there.

So there it was: "Steal the girl…"

Now I am not what you would call naïve, but at this point I might have thought for a moment about the wiles of the devil. You see he can set the table in such a way as to attract the individual for whom he has a plan by offering up a plate that creates an appetite just perfectly particular to that person's palate. In this case the menu had for an appetizer "beautiful and wounded mourning dove in need of rescue," for the main course, "arrogant, cruel, and prideful captor needing to be taken down," and for dessert, "the sweet forbidden fruit of the rescued treasure served à la mode with a big scoop of job well done."

Oh yeah, he had found a way to get me to compromise my principles by using my principles, to forgo what is right in an eternal sense, a spiritual sense for what is right in an immediate, right here and now "She needs help and who is there but me?" kind of sense. Which if I had not been smitten would have made absolutely no sense. Alas, as I have made clear I had no experience with women. I mean, did she even *want* to be rescued?

Well, I thought that was a question that could possibly be answered with a little imaginative maneuvering on my part.

"You know, Coyote, I don't think you and Gator are going to be very good friends and now look what you've done…He's gonna have to change over to a jockey shift 'cuz there's not enough pulling power in that hand to work a clutch for sure."

That comment was interpreted as an approving admiration for what he had done and I saw the corners of his eyes, and under the big beard the corners of his mouth betray a satisfied smile. Flattery would definitely be a useful tool in dealing with this megalomaniac. And that made perfect sense since every move he made was by design a fishing expedition—the bait, all his cool stuff. What he hoped to catch was a trophy-size issue of "Man we're all so impressed!"

"Like I said, I won't tolerate a thief of any kind."

I thought:

Yeah, except the kind of thief that steals a beautiful woman from the world where she could be bringing light to the tired eye as she simply walks down the street, as she smiles at the old broke-down Korean War vet sitting at the bus stop, off to the V.A. for his chemo and he catches a glimpse and a whiff of that sweet tropical fragrance, and for a moment he is transported back to the days when his back was straight and his jaw was set, his virility an aura that he wore with nobility. Except the kind of thief that steals from a flower the light and rain it needs to survive and is held instead in a dark prison of his wicked lust and his hands that bring only pain and fear. Yeah, you won't tolerate a thief of any kind except the kind you are: a thief of light and life.

"I hear ya! Hey, I gotta take a leak and it's way past time for a fix, plus I kinda wanna see why you've done with inside of this place. The outside is biker paradise, bro, my curiosity is killin' me!"

Coyote was looking at me, weighing possible ramifications of allowing me through the threshold into the inner sanctum. He looked from me to the Packard and back to me again. I may have been a completely strung-out hype but I was also a biker and as such I had to project an image of strength. Like I said, yeah, I was a hope-to-die dope fiend but our crew was bucks up; we made bank. Those little twenty-thousand-dollar paydays like I described with Moose and Ronnie were not unusual. Frog, Moose, John Curry, and I had a little prison yard weight pile in the backyard with an Olympic Bench, a dip station, a pull-up station, a couple of curl bars, and some dumbbells. We'd spend hours out there, being wired, pounding protein shakes, smoking reds, and pumping iron.

Standing there before Coyote I knew how I looked. I was sinewy, muscular, wearing a brand-new white wife beater, crisp indigo Levi Bells, Chippewa engineer boots with horseshoe taps (letting them run along the asphalt at freeway speed sent a trail of sparks into the night air), a handmade belt with a big single-wing Harley buckle also handmade by a brother in Canon City Prison in Colorado. On my hip was a straight-blade Schrade, the sheath tooled by the same leatherman as the belt. I was put together. I didn't look like some garage dwelling tweaker (those days were coming, though).

Parked at the curb was a 1954 Packard Clipper, sea foam green with a black top, impossibly tall white walls, the whole thing lowered only two inches just to give it "stance" without compromising the period correctness of design perfection that was the '50s Packard. We had the projected insanity of the Black House, doorless, heartless, looking like a haunted house more than anything, but individually each of us had a certain style. In the backyard of the Black House was a sheet-metal structure that betrayed the truth about the prosperity of the tribe: a '57 Stingray, a '71 El Camino big block Super Sport, an early Porsche bathtub Speedster—those were just kind of ours. Besides the Packard I had a white '51 five-window Chevy pickup, bone stock. Every one of those cars was the pinnacle representation of its breed.

Where were we? Oh yeah. So Coyote was checking me out. All I wanted to do was get inside and see if I could see in Sunshine some desire to be set free.

CHAPTER 15

"Yeah, man, let's go on in. Uh, I heard you might travel with a little slow and scratchy. I've never done it but I hear that yer speedballs are pretty amazing."

He said this quietly, conspiratorially, as if we might be overheard discussing a matter of National Security. He could only have gotten this information from Moose.

"I might have a balloon or two in Rosie."

"Rosie? Oh, yer 'fifty-four...Can I take a closer look at that sweetheart? She is a rare and beautiful bird."

I have to confess, pride welled up in me. There were always a lot of cool cars out there on the road but mostly Chevys, Fords, the occasional Merc or Pontiac, but my baby was unusual, and she was perfect in every way. Showroom perfect. So then, this matter of the clandestine delivery of his request for a little heroin. The scooter tramp world and its peculiar prejudices. I had seen things done, ingested, abused, perpetrated, forced, stolen, coerced, seduced, and all with the mind-set that "We do whatever the hell we want!"

Yet you allow that you shoot a little dope, heroin, and you are out of the car, shunned, dis-fellowshipped, and talked about. Unless, of course, you have a dump truck load of power and strength, in which case they may still talk about you but it will be in hushed tones and with guilt-infected shifty glances, afraid of discovery. But it never failed. It was amazing how often a transaction with a biker would be punctuated or ended with this very same top secret request.

"I haven't slept in a week and my teeth are down to the nubs from grinding and I hear you have the magic 'slow me down.'" Or as Coyote put it, which by the way was pretty darn original, "a little slow and scratchy."

Nice, I liked that.

But me? I have come over from the other side of the tracks so many times, the Sureno side, the Brown Pride side, where just the opposite is in full effect.

Over there they shun the teeth-grinding, paranoid, imagining of scenarios that don't exist and those who turn those imagined scenarios into expressions of mistaken retaliation and campaigns based on a delusion created in the mind that is sleep deprived, protein bankrupt, and poorly equipped to fight the powers of suggestion that come out of the dark places, the human heart.

Over there the fidgety, chops-licking, dry-mouth guy bouncing on the balls of his feet is ridiculed, scorned, and quite possibly hurt. If your eyes are pinned and you seem to have an incurable itch, if you are quiet and contemplative in the face of a rumor, slipping into a dark alley or the kitchen table of an "abuelita" as she is making tortillas and pico de gallo to plan your "movida," then you may be deemed trustworthy.

Coyote let himself in Rosie's passenger side and I stood on the curb. It was real, the deep appreciation I could see in his face as he scanned the beautifully sweeping lines of the dash in its ebony excellence. Oh man, in each of us were so many facets. He loved the art, he loved the beauty, that was real and unfeigned. So there was in him a sensitivity to beauty, yet it engendered in him the need to possess. I could also see in him that if he had an opportunity he would take Rosie, finding satisfaction possibly more in the depriving me of my baby than in him actually having her.

That was fine and I was glad I got to see the look on his face that was both appreciative and scheming. I knew at once that I would have very little trouble killing him. He looked up at me with a *Well, what's up?* expression.

Yeah, knucklehead, I'm gonna go to my car stash with you sittin' right here, must have been written all over my face 'cuz I saw the light go on.

"Oh yeah, sorry, man…"

"I'll meet you back at your front door."

I had a stash place in Rosie that was impenetrable, easy to get to but impossible to detect. It held an ammo box. Yeah, I know we use a lot of ammo boxes, but admit it, they are perfect—watertight and, as I discovered on one occasion, somewhat flame resistant. Anyway, in this particular ammo box I kept a roll of duct tape, some zip ties, a bandana, (gag), some crystal, a week's worth of Mexican salt and pepper, and five grand. (You never know when a stroker motor or maybe even a complete bike would present itself for a real good price.) Oh yeah, and a little .38-caliber hammerless revolver and a box of shells. Boy Scout motto is, "Always be prepared." Interestingly I was kicked out of the Scouts for pocketing the money from the sale of Jamboree tickets. Oh, that and selling joints to my pack leader's little snitch kid.

Coyote was standing at the front door and I was really hoping he wouldn't be able to tell that my heart was beating like the drum solo from "In-A-Gadda-Da-Vida." Where was she? Would I see her? Would she see me? Was there any way a chord could have been struck in her? Could this be one of those kismet moments that so far (except Michelle) I had never felt? Two people never speaking and only coming within feet of each other are struck with the lightning bolt of passion, an unspoken moment in which two fates are suddenly intertwined and two lives are melded into one before a word is ever spoken.

"Come on in."

Hesitantly spoken? Not sure. My own fear of discovery manifesting a nonexistent apprehension? Maybe.

The inside of the house was only about half done—lots of boxes still packed, no sense of a home, and that in itself told me all I needed to know. Her heart did not live here.

'Let's go out to the kitchen. It's a little more put together."

I followed him through the cluttered living room and I noticed that while the place had no feel of a home shared by two people who are into what they are doing together it was very clean. In the kitchen the countertops sparkled and the kitchen fixtures did too. There was a heavy, round oak table with four matching chairs. The chairs were oversized, rough hewn, and when Coyote sat in one it enveloped him. I had to fight the urge to see if his feet were on the floor. He really was a small man; maybe I mentioned before about him being five eight. I guarantee if he had known the effect the chair created in regard to his stature he would have had that dining room set out of there lickety-split. From the car I had procured a couple of outfits and two balloons. I figured he could supply the glass since he just came up by a quarter pound.

I didn't know if he had experience with intravenous drug use or not, but we were about to find out. And sure enough, just as I was thinking that he went to the silverware drawer and pulled out a big spoon and then filled a glass of water from the sink.

"Sunshine! Bring a cotton ball or a couple of Q-tips out here!"

In what universe was it cool to talk to your woman like that? Where had he been that he supposed that was going to impress me? Or maybe he didn't care what I thought—she was his possession and he was going to treat her as he pleased.

She came in a hurry and deposited the requested items on the table, both of them, cotton ball and Q-tips. There was no eye contact, no thank-you touch on the arm or the butt, just a cool indifference and an unspoken dismissal. I was beginning to doubt if she was a user. She showed no interest in the drugs that were laid out on the table. She quietly posted up behind Coyote's back but face-to-face with me from across the room. I wanted so desperately to look at her, to communicate somehow, but I knew that he would pick up on it so I just kept her in my sight peripherally, not ever looking at her directly. Oh, but my heart was racing because he had his back to her and she was doing enough communicating for the both of us.

She wasn't waving her arms or mouthing words silently for me to read, no, she stood perfectly still as if Coyote would sense anything else, which I am sure he would have.

But her eyes...

Her eyes were telling me that she had felt the same things in the garage and that there was a smoldering fire in her. Its coals banked for the moment the sweet breeze of freedom blew over her and then it would come alive, it would rage bright and hot, unquenchable. I dared not look at her for more than a second for fear of arousing this creep's suspicion, but I wanted to look at her. I wanted to just stare into those eyes for hours.

Coyote had the quarter pound of product up on the table and he spooned out about a gram or so onto a little piece of polished granite. He slid the spoon, the glass of water, the cotton ball, and the gak toward me and I supposed that meant he wanted to get the show on the road. In my hand I held the two insulin syringes and two balloons of very good chiva. I wondered if it was good enough to kill him.

"So did you say you've never done smack before?"

"No..."

"If you don't mind my asking, why now?"

"Moose and I go way back. Ten years or so when he was out Phoenix way we had a lot of business. He has told me a lot about you. In fact it was me and a couple of partners that bought those Dilaudids you guys lifted in D.H.S. So I know what you're into. Even without Moose there are enough stories about you out there on the outlaw trail. The junkie with juice, compassionate but treacherous, kind but brutal. You can get in anywhere and nobody would ever brace you about your preferred method of delivering drugs to your bloodstream. Runnin' with the same faithful crew year in and year out.

"Anyway I have always been curiously attracted to smack and I'm not about to go looking for it in the Barrio or try to score off some hooker, so when I met you face-to-face earlier I thought, 'Now's my chance.'"

"I guess my reputation precedes me."

"Yeah, so here we are."

He looked at the balloons I had laid on the table with the rigs.

I began to slowly and methodically prepare, bending the spoon so it would lay flat, carefully taking the knots out of the balloons, emptying one into the spoon and then stretching it and allowing it to snap back to loosen what was stuck to the inside. As I prepared I spoke a ritual, a truth. I exposed the mystery.

"Okay, man, so check it out. Heroin is the dirty girlfriend—she's the one who does things for you that no girl ever did before, takes you to places you know no one will ever take you again. She makes every single thing you have ever done look like a mistake because every single thing she does is beyond perfection. Speed pumps you full of ideas, heroin takes all those ideas and throws them in the Dumpster, she takes you to a place where you don't need ideas because everything is already exactly right; she makes it that way. But remember I said she is the dirty girlfriend because you are so into her that you will never cheat, never even look at another, but she will sleep with your best friend right in front of you. If you try to leave her she will ravage your body so mercilessly that you will never try to leave her again. In fact you will spend all your waking hours making sure you always have her right next to you. You love her at first but after she steals every bit of your ability to tell her no you begin to hate her, but you will never leave her. The source may go dry and you will drive a thousand miles to find her. You may get busted and be deprived of her touch as the agony of separation rips into the deepest parts of your body and soul. You will know sickness like you have never known. If you are locked up long enough you will find yourself again and the pain will leave but you will not be free, because as soon as you put your feet on the street you will seek her out.

"You will find her before you do any other thing because she is the only one who can touch you in the deep places. She is a whore but you love her, even though loving her is killing you. All that to say, you asked for a speedball, but this girl you have to meet for the first time alone."

I held the flame of my Zippo under the spoon and that smell filled the room.

Nothing else smelled like heroin cooking. It had a vinegar quality to it and whenever I smelled it my bowels would go all watery and my mouth would begin filling with pre-vomit saliva. It did not make me sick; rather the anticipation was so strong that my body would just begin to want to come out of itself.

Setting the spoon on a napkin so not to mark the table with the sooty black residue of the "cook," I rolled a little ball of cotton and dropped it into the hot mix. Drawing it up it filled the U-100 to the limit. I squirted two-thirds back for myself and handed him the rig. I didn't want to kill him yet. I was curious to see what he would do next. What I had given him should have been enough for a sweet introduction but not an OD.

"Sunshine, get over here!"

My skin crawled at the sound of her name in his mouth, it fouled it so badly.

She knew what to do. She walked up behind him and grasped his bicep in both her hands and gave a light squeeze. He had pipes and he had no trouble slamming and I watched as the plunger rode down the shaft of that rig. I waited, one-two-three, and then it came, the hitch in the breathing, the heavy sigh and the exclamation.

"Oh my God!"

"No, not God, but she would sure like you to think so..."

"What?"

"Nothing, brother, just enjoy."

I had mine ready to go.

"Sunshine"—the first time I said her name—"would you hold me forever?"

What I really said was:

"Sunshine, would you hold me off as well, please?"

She had come to Coyote from behind but she was facing me and so she stood in front of me. She was wearing a Mexican summer dress made of that muslin-like material that is both light and gauzy. It was the kind that had the embroidery around the yoke and shoulders. The bright white of the fabric against her dark skin was so lovely. She was barefoot and as she approached me, reaching out to take my arm between her perfectly sculpted hands, her knee pressed against my thigh. At the same time she took my arm in her hands and a wisp of ebony hair brushed against my face.

She was over and above me and I could both feel and smell her breath, like a warm sea breeze during a lemon, tangerine, and raspberry sunset, like lavender tea with cream and honey. I did my fix and she stepped away quickly but not before both of us discharged a jolt of electricity so powerful her knees went weak. She reached to steady herself on the table and for a moment I was very afraid for her, but as she stepped away and gave me a clear view of her captor relief flooded me. He was in that private place only the bad girlfriend can take you and they were very much alone there. But I had had one second of another place and it was a place I had never been. Even the shot of chiva I had just done did nothing to calm my racing heart. I would do anything for this. I would change my life.

Coyote was lost in a nod and for a moment I thought I had given him too much; I wished I had given him even more. How easy that would have been, the whole balloon would certainly have wrung the last breath out of his chest. I had thought, as I watched him covet Rosie with such dirty lust over another man's treasure, it would be easy to kill him but killing is a thing that is very different in the mind than it is in reality. In a fantasy, in "Imagine If Land," you never see the life actually leave the body. You never see how desperately the living being fights to keep living. You never see the terror, the absolute horror as the dying one begins to lose the fight and life begins to slip away. Of course in the overdose there is no fight, no realization that life is being taken, only the sweet bliss of the deep swoon. Then the horror probably comes later when you awaken to the torment and heat of hell because you died a godless, self-serving drug addict. The realization that all you heard about God is true and the god you served was an idol.

The Bible says, "The life is in the blood." The junkie every day and every night dilutes that life-carrying blood with the god of death disguised as a whisper of heaven in a syringe. Heroin is an idol that demands sacrifice every four hours and failure to comply exacts immediate and severe consequences.

We both looked at Coyote and the very real possibility that he was pretending to be in a nod lost its fight with the desperate need we felt to somehow convey our newly discovered and very secret truth. She reached over and as gently as a butterfly wing she placed the palm of her hand on my face and I reached up and covered her hand with mine. Her lips silently formed the word, "Soon!"

I looked at her in such a way as to etch her portrait into my mind so deeply that a thousand years could not erase it. Her hair was so black it shot arrows of cobalt blue into the atmosphere when the light hit and it framed her face perfectly. Her eyes literally sparkled like emeralds. I had never seen a green so deep but in the deepest part of that green were tiny flecks of gold making a perfect circle surrounding the pupil and causing the iris to glow ethereally. Her full red lips needed no color and they seemed to be always parted ever so slightly revealing impossibly white teeth. She was brown and in such a way as to pull all of the light out of the air and shoot it back out at you with a warmth that made me think of being under an outpouring of caramel. She had a dancer's body, trim and lithe, like a deer running through the forest at full speed, not being pursued but just for the joy of the running. I had only heard her speak once and that was in the garage when she came out to announce Gator's request for an audience with Coyote. I never wanted to hear her say "I'm sorry" Again, but I wanted to hear her speak every day for the rest of my life.

Enough, then. Every second that we were near each other was a deeper danger that our chemistry would betray us.

"Yo, Coyote, I gotta go!"

He was instantly awake and way too alert. Had he been playing possum? Was he testing Sunshine's loyalty?

"What about that speedball, man?"

"I'm leavin' this other balloon. Cook up half, the way I did, and then add glass to taste. None of my business but do you slam all your go-fast?"

"As quiet as it's kept, yeah, I do."

"Then maybe add a little bit more than your regular dose so you get a good jolt."

No, he suspected nothing. In fact it was looking as if he wanted to be my friend. I could see why. Outwardly our styles were very compatible. We both cared about making money more than we cared about much else, though for very different reasons. He cared about money for his identity and he was all about the appearance of things. I liked to look good not because I cared what people thought but because I was deeply afraid of being one of the walking dead, the cotton beaters, the ones that shot their dope in the dirty, disease-ridden rest room at the corner gas station. I knew myself well enough to know that if I took my eyes off the prize for even a second I would lose my courage. I would lose the heart that it took to pull the kinds of scams we pulled. Money meant I never had to use the same syringe twice. Money meant I could stay at the Marriot and not the Fire Station Motel or the Caravan Inn. Nice cars and crisp new jeans announced my solvency to the world. You see, I didn't care if people thought I was dangerous or crazy, daring or courageous, I only cared that if they thought those things then I was widely separated from my biggest fears. My biggest fear was being dope sick in an alley, penniless and without a single good idea. A dead man walking, weak and vulnerable to anyone and anything.

Yeah, I could see how outwardly Coyote might think we were cut from the same cloth. But he looked at Rosie my '54 Packard Clipper with eyes that would take it from me if he could. Until today I had never seen in the possession of any man anything that I wanted to take for my own. So I wondered, maybe I even agonized over the course of action I should take. If I played to his attraction to me and made him my friend to get to Sunshine was it any less a crime than him wanting what I had and if the opportunity arose taking it from me.

I was given to the Sir Galahad position in that I was not stealing but performing a rescue. The other approach was in the short term the more dangerous because it called for announcing my thoughts about him right from the start, basically a robbery as opposed to a stealthy burglary done from the inside.

"I'm taking her and I hope you don't like it!"

I knew very little about him, who he knew, how much of him was real and how much was hyperbole. Moose! Yeah that was it…Before I made any kind of plan I need to put some well-thought-out but serious questions to the big man.

There were two distinctly separate but equally pressing issues. First the freedom of this beautiful girl, and second a very glamorous and colorful revenge for Gator. Briefly I wondered if those dogs would eat their master. Well, we'd figure it out soon enough.

Moose and I had been down the trail and back up more than a few times and I knew he cared for me. The fact that he had told Coyote all about me and yet had never once even mentioned this little man's existence to me spoke volumes about where his favor was stored. Then what did he know about Sunshine? Had he known her before as well? Where did she come from? How did she end up with him?

CHAPTER 16

The Black House...I had to drive by the front of the pad to get to the alley in the back where the car barn was. It was a disheveled, unkempt place. Flat black from stem to stern without a single living thing on the premises, but it was a fully equipped compound. Impenetrable perimeter fence supported by two large dogs, the car barn containing a lift and the tools to accomplish any project a motorhead might dream up, a little outdoor pig-iron weight pile with all you needed to stay yoked up.

It literally screamed, "Don't mess around with this place!"

I was always content there, it reflected my life, dark, dead, but very effective and displaying not even a nod toward fitting in with the world. Oh, but there is something about being exposed to beauty when you hadn't seen it, thought about it, or cared about it in so long that it was as remote as the landscape of the moon. Driving past the front of the house it suddenly took on the appearance of sunbaked roadkill. Mercilessly abandoned, forgotten and stenchy, fumes of death rising off of it in waves almost tangible, visible.

I stopped Rosie and put her in park, shut her down and just sat there. For the first time in a very long time I thought about God. You see, I was constantly surrounded with darkness, it was just normal. The smell of a piss- and puke-drenched alley had long since ceased to offend. That is the way of sin in this world at any level. What may have at one time been offensive or made a person feel a measure of trepidation after continual exposure just becomes the status quo. At one time, even several times in my life, I had been in possession of a sweet spot, a relationship with my creator, the most recent having been my summer with Craig and Leslie at Big Calvary. But in a single moment, a moment with no thought of holiness and no fear of consequences, I had yet again thrown in my lot with the wicked and now the place of the wicked was just the zip code I lived in.

But the perception of sweet and seemingly unsullied beauty, especially a beauty that is in bondage to ugliness…well, it seems it can often be the herald calling out the arrival of a remembrance. A remembrance of God…

The Bible says about the saved person that He has called us out of darkness and conveyed us into the kingdom of the Son of His love, and yet I, the proverbial rope in a tug-of-war between God and Satan, had lent my pitiful excuse for strength in pulling for the side of the enemy.

The stark contrast between the stink of death surrounding this compound and the lavender and cream of the breath coming from Sunshine had caused a cacophony of conflict to awaken in me. Like Peter seeing the face of Jesus and realizing that he had, in fact, denied the Lord, I also wept bitterly.

And then He was there for the first time in a very, very long time: *"I love you, my child, and I will always be with you."*

I could feel Him, I could really feel Him almost like the first time as I walked with my horse Maya past the cathedral in Puerto Vallarta and witnessed the worship of an ancient woman as she made her way on her knees up the coarse sandstone steps leading to the great doors. It was Ash Wednesday, I was eight years old, and had been made the plaything of a man who I had trusted as a mentor, and I was in so deep that the marrow of my bones quaked with fear.

That was the first time He came to me and through the years He had reappeared in my dark moments or in times of gravity.

But then, I had to slam on the brakes because while I may have been overly sensitive I was also supremely rebellious and stubborn so I shook off the moment, put on my tough-guy costume, and fired Rosie up. She was period correct and in addition to the tall rims and a very slight lowering job she had an exhaust system with serious authority, and it always gave me a rush. By the time I got around the corner to the back entry I was fully Eddie again, and behold, I spy, I spy with my little eye the '71 Catalina gangster mobile, aka Moose's war chariot, parked in the yard. Perfect!

Moose had a crooked grin on his face and I knew it was because Moose loved a good drama and this had the makings of an earth shaker.

"He bought her."

"What do you mean 'he bought her'?"

"Slave trade, bro, wake up!"

"Bought her from who and where and when?"

"Couple of years ago from some cartel dude in Nogales, she was sixteen or seventeen then but I think he has her as twenty-one on her driver's license. You know he did the whole dead kid's birth certificate thing. Haha. Her last name is Walker. First time I ever saw a half Chinese-half Mexican named Walker. Come to think of it, first time I saw a half Chinese-half Mexican, period. Though ya know she just has to have some white girl in the mix 'cuz her nose is just too straight and too perfect to be all Asia-Mex. Her birth certificate reads Loretta Walker. She looks about as much like a Loretta Walker as I look like Loretta Lynn. Thus she is called Sunshine and that fits real good, don'tcha think? In fact lemme ask ya, what are you thinkin' 'cuz you got that deep crack of concentration right in the middle of your forehead about now."

I said nothing but my body language and my eyes told a story.

"Oh man, bro, are you serious?"

He looked at me for a long moment and I knew that he was going through everything he knew about me and weighing his next statement, because it would certainly be representative of his position in it all.

"Yeah, man, you know what? She's good and he's not and these last, and now that I'm thinkin' about it it's been three years almost exactly, these last three years have been all the way wrong. He treats her like he does one of his tools or a pair of boots and she has the heart of the faithful in her for the right guy. I ain't sayin' that's you, but you'd be a hell of an improvement for certain sure!"

"So who is this guy?"

"Well he is certainly to be taken seriously because has a wicked temper and he ain't afraid to display it."

"Yeah, I saw an example of that today…He accused Gator of stealing an S&S carb off of his workbench."

"Then what happened?"

"He asked Gator to fetch a box down off the shelf over the workbench and when he did Coyote whipped out that big bowie and quicker that a rattler strikes he lobbed three fingers off of Gator's left hand."

"No way, yer kidding, right?"

"Then he threw Gator's fingers to his dogs."

"What did you do? What did Gator do?"

"It happened so fast there wasn't much I could do and Gator, he just got out of there as fast as he could. But I played like I barely knew him and it was none of my business anyway, but I'll tell you what I'm cooking up one really good idea about payback. First we gotta get Shine out of there."

"Oh, Shine is it, now?"

"Shut yer pie hole stupid!"

"Yeah, okay, Romeo, but let me get this straight: Are you going from practicing bachelorhood as a religion to playing house, like, overnight?"

"Yeah, I guess that's what's happening."

"Okay, I'm in. Like I said he's got a temper, but that actually plays in your favor because he's got no friends, bro, virtually none. Some business associates, yeah, but nobody that's gonna side up with him in a skirmish."

"I thought you guys had a little crew down there in Phoenix."

"Well here's the thing. He was always a loner, really arrogant and aloof, and so he never made friends and gave the impression of being more important than everyone else. Serious Napolean complex. A couple of years ago a bunch of indictments came down for manufacturing and weapons stuff and he was a key player, but also one of the only people who didn't get indicted. Two other guys who figured big in the whole movida also escaped indictment but it came out later they were rats and one of them was actually an officially employed confidential informant for the DEA. There was never any way to connect Coyote as a rat and I know for a fact that he was clean or I wouldn't still be making moves with him, but his popularity ship has sailed with everybody who is anybody in Arizona and Mexico. All his biz is now up Vegas way and other parts of Nevada and some in Colorado but he has no face, no influence. He's just a guy with some products for which there is a good demand. All alone in this big old world. What I am sayin' is it is solely you and him dog."

"See here's the thing. Yer OC bred, lifelong tribe member. It is just him and he can't stand up against your heritage. So I'm thinkin' why don't we take a couple of the fellas and, say, a pound of gak and inform him that there has been a transfer of ownership on the property called Miss Sunshine. No negotiations, done deal. Maybe throw in a discount price on future investments and that way it's more business and less personal."

" I have a pound but it's Robin's. I have the cash to buy it from her but she's been real careful about distribution and has been keeping all her sales to quarter elbows and watching their trails to determine a flow chart kind of thing. She wants to watch the effects of her product on the market without making too big of an impact on the club side of the biz. She's sly and smart."

"Yeah but she also really wants you all the way in and she knows she doesn't have you, but she needs you to really have the loyalty of the rest of the tribe. She has their attention because she has the best dope anybody has ever seen, but they all still look to you. Maybe if she did you a favor she could get some reciprocation from you in the form of an allegiance."

"So yer sayin' basically to sell my soul to the evil enchantress—actually the devil. Because you might not see it but it is clear to me that is exactly who she works for. And I don't mean in some allegorical sense, it's as real as real can get."

"You know I don't take stock in all that 'eternal good and its war with the powers of darkness junk,' but I do know life is short. Just how bad do you want her, bro?"

"I guess I want her more than I have ever wanted anything, brother. Something happened and at first I thought it was just me, but it was both of us I'm sure and I know I can't let it go. By hook or by crook I gotta get her outta there and see what the future holds. I could see making some big changes in the way I live maybe…"

"Well I guess that is going to depend on the deal you make with Stevie Nicks, ain't it? By the way, she's in the house with Frog right now. You wanna go and brace her with this?"

"We could just bypass Robin and take some of the boys over and take her."

I thought to myself, *In fact, we're gonna do something like that but Sunshine will already be gone. We're gonna do something later for Gator. Later for Gator.* I chuckled.

"What's so funny?"

"Nothing, bro."

"So we could do somethin' like that except that there would be blood and what was intended as a simple two-one-one, armed robbery, could quickly become a one-eighty-seven, murder one, and what if the one killed was yer objective, yer prize, yer treasure? Bullets fly wild with short barrels and shorter tempers. Passion and accuracy are never in the same gunfight."

"Look, man, before we go any further we gotta call the Port and find out what's going on with Gator. We gotta convince him to freeze on taking any action because I have an idea, and if we do it right this tribe will come up and Gator will be riding high."

"Okay. I'll call the Port, you deal with the dark princess."

"True that, bro, let's go inside."

The place was dark, not physically but spiritually, even more so now that Robin was a full-time resident. I thought that if I brought in a house-plant it would be dead in a day. By now all the pets had been replaced. Frog even found somebody who sold us some choice, fat Western diamondbacks. I wasn't immune to the insanity. I still liked to do a big speedball with Frog and milk those snakes for venom. We kept it in the fridge like a new mom stored breast milk. I tried to imagine bringing Sunshine into this place and then I thought:

Sunshine is exactly what this place needs!

My room had the biggest windows and faced southwest and got the most light. Frog's dungeon had the windows painted black, was all mirrors and a disco ball with a king-sized bed, a couch, an armoire that was his armory, and a desk with a bright tensor light, for the rare occasions he needed light, like doing a shot or weighing out product. Scary stuff went on in there, I could often hear it. I knocked on his door.

"Hey, Dirty Legs, you got a minute?"

Robin and I had come to a place of friendly antagonism, all said with a smile but with both of us knowing that the backgammon game we were playing had deadly consequences. It was only a matter of time. We were smiling enemies and I was about to make a major concession of pieces to her side of the board.

"I'm coming, Sir Galahad!"

I knew then that she knew. I don't know how she knew but she knew, but I wasn't surprised. She had from the beginning known things there was no natural way for her to know.

I went into my room and opened up all the windows and drew all the shades, letting in as much light as possible. She emerged from their lair and immediately her hands flew up to her eyes and she abruptly turned around and ran back in the dungeon. When she came out again she was wearing a pair of Wayfarers. I was laughing my butt off.

"Aren't you supposed to catch fire or melt or something?"

"Yeah, whatever…So you, Young Edward, are going to rescue the fair damsel and you need my assistance."

She always called me Young Edward to remind me of how I had destroyed Hope with heroin after Wayne's murder in Mexico. Hope always called me Young Edward in her Victorian accent, with that beautiful smile playing on her lips and it always succeeded in jolting me. But how had Robin even known about Hope or the girl at Cook's Corner or any of it? How did she know about Sunshine?

Well, I knew how she knew and yet I was still prepared to do business.

But by her calling me Young Edward she was pointing directly at my failure to protect Hope and projecting yet another future failure would soon come to pass. I could only hope she was wrong but somewhere deep inside I suspected she was right. A deal that starts with a dark deed rarely comes out an ode to joy.

"Yeah, that's about the size of it."

"And so you need a sizable weight of The Quicksilver, correct?"

"Yep, that's it."

"You know my methods and their wherefores and whys, so how do you propose to actuate this transaction without upsetting the balance I have set in place?"

"I will give Coyote a pound on a onetime basis, on his word that he will take it out of state, and I will offer him a discount on his quarter-pound price, which will come out of my pocket for a predetermined amount of purchases."

"Eddie, I applaud your bravado and I am prepared to give you two pounds, gratis: one you may give him as part of the initial transaction and the second you can use for his future quarter-pound purchases. If I were you I would limit it to four, but hey, that's your business. This is going to be so much fun on so many levels as a spectator, and frankly I am dying to see how you are with a woman. And since I assume she will be residing here in the mansion with us I will have a firsthand opportunity to see you in action. Maybe you can put flower boxes on the front porch. But, Eddie, don't get a kitten or a puppy, one might accidentally fall into a snake cage. So if you are ready to deal I have your product all ready to go and a document for you to sign. Okay, Eddie?"

"Yeah, Stevie, let's let her rip!"

She hated being called Stevie Nicks.

She came out of the dungeon with an ancient-looking scroll and I thought:

Really, are you kidding me right now?

She sat down at the table by the window in my room and rolled it out. Suddenly the room felt cold and there was a smell like ether and smoke.

It went like this:

I, Eddie Wilkens, hereby transfer all rights to my everlasting soul to the serpent of Genesis, the son of the morning of Isaiah, the nemesis of all that is true and good, the ultimate hater of God, Satan the prince of this world. And in exchange I will be repaid in power and authority, influence and strength in this world and in this world only, but my eternity belongs to the father of hell, the king of demons, Luciifer. I understand that in this life, in this world I will be a triumphant king, but in the next life I will have endless torment.

In my blood,

Eddie Wilkens

I read it and I didn't flinch.

In her hand she had an ancient feather quill, a small crystal saucer, and a syringe.

"Give me your arm and hold yourself off, Eddie."

I did as she instructed and she went to my ditch and filled the syringe. She immediately squirted into the dish. Holding the quill out to me she said simply:

"Sign, Young Edward."

I dipped the quill in my blood and suddenly there He was, and He spoke to me in that same benevolent whisper that He had since I was a child.

"I love you, my child, and I will always be with you."

I couldn't do it, even though I didn't believe I could sell my soul, because in spite of the way I lived I knew that God and I would have our reckoning and that He would emerge in possession of every part of me. Yeah, I knew the truth and I believed the truth, and yet I lived in total disregard for the grace that had been extended to me. Every single day I disrespected the sacrifice He made to save me from the very things that I was forever drawing closer into my life. I was really nailing Him to that cross every day, over and over. If the truth was known I wept most every night and those alone moments when I was relatively straight were moments of a deep self-loathing as I came face-to-face with my own hypocrisy, my own pathetic lack of character.

The only solutions available to me were either to get clean and find my way back to the doors of Calvary or to do another shot, commit to another escapade that would temporarily bury the light under a truckload of dirty sin. Take me to the place of a numbness so complete that I could no longer feel and take me to a place of sinister involvement in this life of drugs and crime so that I was too busy watching the safety of my self-made security perimeter. It was a perimeter that I built and guarded to protect me from any affairs involving the heart, too busy watching these things to look up. Except that now I was opening up that perimeter to beauty, opening it up to love, opening it up to a commitment to another person and those were very dangerous propositions, but then as usual I was just going to barge ahead, consequences be damned. At the end of the day I didn't believe it was possible for me to sell something that didn't belong to me. As Robin had said when we first met:

" There is too much God in you, Eddie. He's dim, but He's there."

The Bible says, "And you are not your own? For you were bought at a price; therefore glorify God in your body and in your spirit, which are God's."

I was a million miles from glorifying God in any way, shape, or form but there was still some of Him in me. He still owned too much of me for any part of me to be merchandise to be sold or traded.

"You know what, Robin? It ain't gonna be this easy. And you know what else? Yer gonna do me this favor just on the strength of the fact that you are, for all intents and purposes, my best dog's old lady, that we live in the same house, our dirty laundry all goes in the same hamper so therefore I wash yer panties. And above all you know this is right and it is what I need, and while we are adversaries in one sense there is a great deal that binds us. Besides all of that, as you yourself said it is going to be fun to watch."

She laughed and poured the rest of the blood on the document and then lit it on fire.

"Ashes to ashes and dust to dust...Isn't that something your God would say?"

The room tilted at an impossible angle and then back to the opposite side and my guts rolled over. My decision had upset her balance but she had enough class to let this one go. At the very least this promised to be an adventure and she was a student of the human character—or lack of it, depending on the circumstances. As a spectator this had all the earmarks of being good entertainment.

"Well, Eddie, I don't get you this time but at some point I will for sure. So for now we might as well get high."

She had two preloaded syringes and she handed me one and I just went to the ditch with it. The last thing I remember was falling back on my bed as shadows gathered around me. I didn't know if it was my housemates, Robin, Frog, and Moose or who, but then I didn't care.

The sound of voices and sunlight coming through the window woke me up and the first thing I saw was five tightly wrapped packages on the table by my window. A pound in one and four quarter-pound packages, all lying neatly in the morning light. It had been about sunset when I did that last shot and here it was morning. Well, after all, I had been up for a long, long time.

I could smell coffee and pot. Pot? Who smoked pot? I hit the head and then I headed for the kitchen and a surprise. Gathered around the table were Frog, Moose, Robin, Johnny Curry, and Gator—missing three fingers—and two other guys from the Port 17 bar, Timmo and Mexican George, both of whom I had known for a very, very long time. I was looking at the perfect crew for part two of my big production. They didn't know it but they were about to get a big issue of fun with a profit.

Frog handed me a cup of coffee.

"Fixed it up just like you, light and sweet."

"Hardy-har-har. I'll be right back."

I went in my room and snapped a balloon of brown into the cooker and then sprinkled some Quicksilver across the top. Scratched some matches on the seat of my 501s and cooked it up a tad.

"Good morning, beautiful world!"

I went back to the kitchen and found the boys going over their weaponry. The air was alive with speed, adrenaline, and barbarism, but man that pot stunk up the place. I knew Mexican George was the culprit.

CHAPTER 17

Moose called the meeting to order:

"Yo, guys, pipe down. I'm gonna call him…"

I was watching Gator, not at all sure bringing him along was wise except for the fact that it would cement in Coyote's mind the OC tribe's solidarity.

When we were at his house yesterday Gator and I had barely acknowledged each other because Coyote's dramatic little production had been the center of attention. I had never seen Coyote at the Port, which was the local watering hole for all the outlaws in OC and I was there at least three times a week. On any given night there would be a hundred bikes lined up in the front ridden by a hundred guys who all knew each other; outsiders were tolerated but not embraced. I am not certain that Coyote even knew the place existed, but if the bar phone rang and a local boy needed help that place would puke out its patrons quick. And they would come with thunder. I was looking at Gator's left hand, a big old bat of gauze bandage with just a little seepage of blood at the end. Clean for the most part. But it was Gator's right hand that interested me most because it was holding a .45 Desert Eagle—a heavy, thunderous hand cannon.

"Gator, my brother! That all happened so quick yesterday, whack and you were gone, wasn't much I could do!"

"Yeah, I know Eddie, it ain't yer fault. Besides I did take that S&S but I don't think it should have cost me those fingers. He is just such an arrogant punk I just wanted to take somethin' from him."

"So what is your plan with that cannon!"

"Oh look, Eddie, I'm just here for support. This is your deal—I'm not gonna mix my biz up with yours. I'll get him in a vulnerable moment one day. I just wanna see this operation, ya know? Is that cool, Eddie?"

"Yeah, Gator. Uh, come with me for a minute, would ya?"

He followed me into my bedroom.

"You wanna do a shot, Dog?"

"With a little brown in it?"

"Yeah, if that's what you favor."

"It will sure help with the throbbing in this paw."

I watched him geeze and I hadn't noticed how much tension from pain was in his face until suddenly it disappeared.

"Oh man, oh man, that feels sooo much better. Thanks, Eddie."

"No sweat, bro. Listen, Gator, we gotta get Sunshine out of there this morning, but if you can trust me a plan is coming together in my head that will see you well compensated for yer paw. You just gotta give me a day or two to work it out."

"I've seen you guys, ya know. You, Frog, and Moose pull off some righteous scams, so yeah, I trust you, Eddie!"

"Okay, brother, but for now just keep it on the down low, and if anyone asks just say you gotta heal up before you even think about it. By the way, how are you gonna ride?"

"Chico and Danny Mac hooked up a suicide shifter for me yesterday...Always wanted one, anyway."

We went back out to the meeting and Moose called us to order.

He picked up the phone and waved us to silence.

"Yeah, Coyote, Moose. Listen, Hoss, me and Eddie are gonna swing by with a little proposition, that cool with you? Okay, then, see ya in about fifteen.

"So, okay let's meet at the Chevron on the corner of Beach and Garden Grove; his pad is about two blocks from there. Me, Eddie, and Robin will go in and in five minutes you all just ride down and park in front of his house. Have a smoke and be cool, just like you were hangin' in front of the Port, got it? I'll give you directions to the pad once we get to the gas station."

Moose, Robin, and I went in the Catalina; everybody else rode. And after we directed everyone to the house from the gas station the three of us went on in.

Coyote was standing in his doorway, hands on hips when we pulled up. He was a fine-looking man, just in miniature, and I had to chuckle. But it also went a long way to explaining why he was the way he was. Except for the hair, the beard, and the shotgun cradled in the crook of his arm he looked like a little kid standing there.

The dogs were nowhere to be seen and he waved us in through the gate.

"Who's the chick?"

Robin pushed herself to the front of our trio and stepped into the doorway, kind of forcing Coyote to take a step back, which unnerved him noticeably.

"Coyote, my name is Robin. I am Frog's lady and I just wanted to get out of the house this fine morning, so I insisted these boys bring me along. They trust me implicitly and so should you."

She had her hand out and whether he wanted to or not he took it and when he did the little boy I imagined in the doorway actually appeared. I suddenly thought of a story Frog had told me a couple of days earlier about how he and Robin had been blasting down Beach Boulevard just passing the Slater Slums, doing an easy sixty. Frog packin', both of them lit, and a cop pulls out of a driveway and races to catch up. He hit the lights and chirped the siren and pulled alongside. He looks over and sees Robin and she shoos him away with her hand. He got this dumb childlike grin and just drove away.

The little-boy Coyote said:

"Come on in."

I had a snapshot vision of the Martinez kitchen with Richard sitting at the table, a drop of blood leaking from his arm:

"*Mi vida loca.*"

"Yeah, brother, my crazy life, could it get any crazier? Nah, don't think so."

I would soon have reason to revisit that thought from a very different perspective.

Coyote led us through the front room and back to the kitchen where we had slammed the day before and gestured to the chairs around the table.

"Have a seat. So you said you had a proposition."

I pulled out the pound and kerchunked it down on the table. A pound of the Quicksilver was really something to behold, even covered in plastic.

"I want to buy something you have."

The little boy seemed to have traded places with the regular Coyote and he looked at me shrewdly.

"What might that be?"

"Not a what but rather a who."

Just as I finished dropping that little bomb the thunder of four sets of straight pipes came blasting down the street. Four black scooters pulled up at the gate and backed into the curb.

"What is this?"

Coyote jumped up from the table and went to look out the door since there were no windows on the front side of the house.

"Is that Gator? What the hell is going on here?"

"Yeah, that's Gator, but don't sweat nothin', Dog, he's just here in the capacity of one of the OC crew getting ready to go to brunch to celebrate. We told those guys to meet us here and then after we made this purchase from you we're all gonna go to brunch to celebrate."

Moose was trying hard to control himself because as I said he finds drama hysterically funny.

"So this is about my woman then, is it?"

At this point I had to take the reins.

"Well, it seems that she might be your property but she was never your woman and this ain't Phoenix or Nogales. You have a choice: you can take a pound of the finest speed ever cooked and a fifty percent discount on the next four quarter-pound purchases you make. This is the first and only time we will let a pound go as a whole unit. You do that, let her walk, and you are free to stay here in OC as your base of operations—but you will conduct no business locally. And so you know, those four brothers are the teeny tip of a very big iceberg. Of course your future as far as Gator is concerned is another matter; that move was unwise. He is born and bred and very well liked."

"I didn't even know you knew him when you were both here yesterday."

"Yeah, well, what can I say?"

"What if she doesn't want to go?"

Robin had vaporized without anyone even noticing but just then she emerged from down the hall carrying a suitcase, and there was Sunshine right behind her with another suitcase and a duffel bag.

"Oh but I do want to go, very much. Your touch is greasy and repulsive and you are very small in every way."

Coyote jumped to his feet and reached for that Rigid Bowie, but Robin had a .25-cal, four-shot derringer leveled at him from a range of less than ten feet. Even at ten feet it would be easy to miss with that little piece but with four shots, well the odds were in the favor of the .25. He sat down and exhaled loudly.

"Do all these people know you're a junkie?"

By now everyone was inside and everyone laughed raucously.

Gator said:

"Man, the whole world knows! And maybe one person cares, that being his mama!"

"You know, Coyote, I have been admiring that Rigid. Would you make a gift of it to me, please? No, actually, let me offer you a trade."

I reached into the pocket of my chambray shirt and pulled out a cigarette cellophane that held ten balloons of Martinez's chiva secured with a rubber band.

"All that 'Does everybody know you're a junkie?' sounds pretty funny after you were so eager to do a shot with me yesterday, but hey, now that the cat is out of the bag with my big secret here's ten bags. Now give me that knife and try not to kill yourself with this much of the bad girlfriend in your hands at one time—or actually, go ahead, kill yourself!"

I wasn't going to display any emotion in this "transaction," but thinking about the bruises on Shine and the fingers no longer on Gator I just got a little hot.

Robin and Shine had hauled her stuff out to the Catalina so there was nothing left to do but roll out. We left Coyote standing in the doorway looking small and confused, probably because Robin had went up and touched his cheek and whispered something to him that seemed to take him back to that little puppy of a Coyote.

I was embarrassed when we rolled into the yard at the Black House and I carried all of Shine's stuff in to my room, looking around at the depraved way we lived. The first thing I said as she followed me in to the room and shut the door was, "I'm sorry about this."

"Don't ever say that to me again!" And she jumped into my arms. "You are all I need, Eddie."

I really hoped so.

CHAPTER 18

She didn't get high. Amazing peace came from her. She was still, deep water. Her name fit her perfectly. Her touch was like the stroke of a dove's wing. I had never, ever been to this place and I was prepared to go to any lengths to keep it. About a week after she came the phone rang and it was Coyote.

"I need one of those quarter elbows."

"Right now?"

"Right now."

"I'm on my way."

I told Shine I was leaving for a bit.

"Eddie, there is some stuff I need at the store. Do you trust me to drive, to go out alone?"

I looked at her standing in a shaft of sunlight that was coming in the window and I trusted her with everything. I trusted her with my life.

"Shine, I have to ask. I mean, you don't use drugs and yet here you are with a drug addict and a criminal living in a temple of evil and yet it seems there is nothing but peace in you. What's up with that? I would trust you with my life and yeah, I bought you from Coyote, but I don't own you; you can go anytime you like. I would pay for you to go anywhere you wanted to go."

She put her hand on my shoulder and pushed me down on the bed and she straddled me. She leaned over me in such a way so that her hair framed a little tent with both of our faces inside.

"I don't want to go anywhere, Eddie."

"You see, that's what I don't understand."

"Eddie, I never met my parents. I don't even know where I was born. I don't even know how old I am. The only identifying documents I have are the ones Coyote had made. Loretta Walker, no middle name, born June 5, 1956, making me twenty years old. Am I twenty, am I seventeen? I don't know. I have never been to school, I learned to read from the whores in the houses I was raised in. I fell in love with books because they could take me away. The only things I know about the world I read in books. All I have ever personally seen is abuse. They started selling me six years ago, so according to my fake birth certificate I was fourteen years old. Does that make you disgusted with me, Eddie?"

My arms found their way around her slim little waist and I pulled her close to me.

" There is nothing you could say or do that could ever make me think anything of you other than you are light, you are life, you are the earth, the moon, and the sun to me."

"See, Eddie, that's why I don't want to go anywhere. We have known each other for eight days but from the moment I saw you I knew you and I knew that you too were born out of time. That you were a heart held captive in a world you did not belong in. I think God put us together, Eddie, so that together we could escape the evil that surrounds us. This place, your life, Eddie, they are full of evil but it is not you. You were not born for this, you were born for pure and great things, just like I was not born to be a whore. They were tired of me when Coyote came into the brothel and when he offered to buy me they were happy to see me go. I didn't know where I was going but I knew that someday I would be set free and I would finally get to begin the journey that God had for me. Coyote is a bad man and he hurt me, but with every injury and every night I spent crying silently I knew that I would not be forever held by anger and wickedness. Then you showed up and I knew. You might think I am crazy but God spoke to me a long time ago, when I was very small, and He told me He loved me and that He would be with me."

"Wait! What did you say?"

"There was a man, I was very small. I was living with a very poor family but I was not their child, they were very mean to me. They had their own children and they treated them nicely but they were very mean to me. One night a man came to the door and they sent me into a room with him. He was drunk and he smelled of cigars, whiskey, and stale sweat. His hot, rank breath was all over me and he took my childhood away and he took a very long time to do it and then he just left me lying there. Lying there in twin pools of blood and tears. It was then that I felt God and I was not angry with Him because He came and He held me and the pain went away and I felt safe. He told me He was sorry and that He loved me. He made me feel that it would not always be this way. It was the memory of that moment that has given me hope and strength through everything."

I could hear the phone ringing and then Robin was knocking at my door.

"Yer homeboy is on the phone."

"Would you mind telling him I'm running a little behind but that I'll be there soon?"

"Sure, Eddie, I'll play secretary for you anytime."

"Thanks, Stevie." I turned to Shine. "I'm sorry, babe." (I had never called her that before but it felt good and right. "Please keep talking."

"Well, there were a few more of those incidents, men coming in the night, until one night a man came and gave them some money and took me with him to a house where they did it professionally. It was a couple of years before they made me do it and until then I just cleaned and brought drinks to the customers. That was when I began to learn to read and it saved me. Books were literally my only port of sanity in a completely insane world. But I never forgot God and His promise and I always had hope and now hope has come to me. So you tell me that you would pay for me to go anywhere I wanted to go and I will ask you again, do you trust me to drive and to go out alone? I am asking you that because God has kept His promise and His promise is you and you are my home now, Eddie."

My head was spinning and I was confused, excited and very, very grateful.

I also knew that I had many things to tell this woman and I would tell her tonight.

"Take Rosie and go wherever you need to go and get whatever you need to get. Can you find your way around here?"

She just giggled and bent down and kissed me hard on the lips.

"I could find my way home from anywhere. I just did, didn't I?"

"Yes, you did."

I gave her a roll of bills and headed out in the five-window.

The dogs were in the yard and Coyote was in the shop when I pulled up. I would never forget the sound of those Dobies' jaws clacking shut when they snatched Gator's fingers out of the air. He spoke to them in German again and then said:

"The gate's open come on in."

I tossed the brown paper bag with his Q.T. up on the bench and it landed right next to the crease that bowie left in the surface after it severed three digits from a man's hand. Coyote handed me a banded stack of bills that I stuck in my back pocket.

"Yer not gonna count it?"

"I don't really think I need to, do I?"

"No, you don't, but I gotta ask you something."

I had a feeling this conversation was going to take place and I was ready for it. I was also very ready for anything that might transpire if it escalated. So he asked me something.

"So how is that stuff—sweet, right? I mean, she was professionally trained, after all."

I had to laugh at the shallow nature of this idiot and I was done with the pretense. If the gloves were gonna come off they might as well come off right now. I knew I was tougher, smarter, and better than this cockroach in a hip, slick, and cool biker disguise. As I stood there looking at this punk I began to wonder. I could see he could build a bike, but could he even ride? Had he ever ridden across three states without stopping just to get to the funeral of a friend? Had he ever gone for a couple of years with only a rigid stroker for transportation? Could he knock on the door of the Hessians Clubhouse at two in the morning and be offered a place to bunk for the night? Or the Sons Of Silence Clubhouse in Colorado Springs or the Bandidos Clubhouse in Texas?

So I asked him the very things I was thinking and then I continued and as I did he went from small to smaller. But there was a danger in this, I knew, because a deeply offended punk can be a very dangerous punk but I continued with this.

"You know, man—or actually, no, you don't know so I am going to enlighten you but it will probably not resonate with you because you are a soulless poser—but Sunshine may have been with a hundred sloppy fat, stinking losers or maybe a thousand and she's been with you, which is surely worse because you look like a guy who should have some class but you are bankrupt of anything worth notice. So she has had the experience of it all and knows how to pretend at it but now she gets to be loved and that has opened up floodgates of joy in her and in that I am the first. So now that you've had your fun trying to get a rise out of me at her expense just know that the next time anything about her comes out of your mouth I am going to do to your tongue what you did to Gator and I am going to use this very same bowie to do it."

Before I knew it the .38 at the small of my back was out and all up in his grill. I had made a decision.

"This whole thing was done wrong, now that I think about it, so we're gonna change the arrangement."

I felt the beast rising up in me, a rage so pure it was swelling up every muscle in my body, and I thought I was going to shoot him in the head but instead I said:

"Yer done here, man...I'm gonna come back here in a week and if you are still here, if this place isn't completely as empty as a ghost town I will kill you and your dogs and I'll lay claim to everything else you have here, even though I already have the best of all you've ever had."

I couldn't help it, I pulled the trigger right next to his ear, blowing out an eardrum and creasing his scalp with a bullet burn. I picked up the lunch bag and walked out. I didn't look back, I didn't care, I felt bulletproof. Lurking around the southernmost outskirts of my adrenaline-charged brain was a notion that I had just bit off a piece of trouble that might be hard to chew, but then Moose's words echoed in my mind:

"See, here's the thing, yer OC bred, lifelong tribe member. It is just him and he can't stand up against your heritage."

I hit the floor-mounted starter button on my precious '51 five-window and those lakewood pipes rumbled to life. I kerchunked the three on the tree into first, let out the clutch, and whipped a U-ee and I laughed my butt off all the way down the street. Yeah, I was headed for an adventure, I was pretty stinkin' sure.

CHAPTER 19

She had drug an old chair out on the porch., She had flour on her forehead and a big mixing bowl I had never seen before in her lap. The sun was going down and everything had that California gold on it. She glanced up briefly and pushed her hair out of the way with the back of her hand, explaining the flour. She smiled and then went back to mixing with her big wooden spoon, which I was sure we didn't have earlier. I realized it was feeling like around six or six thirty and I had left about three. Evidently we had both gotten a lot done.

When I left the soon to be vacated Coyote compound and realized I had an extra quarter pound of go (Oops, I forgot to give the money back.), I thought it would be good to practice some benevolence and finalize the plan that was bouncing around in my brain. I cruised up to Costa Mesa to the Port. I always loved that little ride down Hamilton and across Brookhurst, over the riverbed and up Victoria into Costa Mesa. It was one of those routes that for some reason connected me to my area. If I had a buck for every time I made that jaunt I'd have a good bit of change. I cruised down Placentia to Seventeenth and over to Newport Boulevard. The Port was just off the corner there. Right across the street there was a Der Wienerschnitzel, probably the only one that stayed open until two a.m. They sold a grip of chili dogs to the bikers who did their only walking in the fifty yards between the front door of the bar and the takeout window of Der Weenie's. There was always a cop posted up there and we all knew each other. Conversations were loose and informal.

"Hey, man, where you guys going tonight?"

"Yer mama's house…"

"Yeah, well, if yer looking for yer old lady I've got her right here in the trunk."

Yuk, yuk, yuk.

I pulled in the driveway and sure enough there was Gator's Knuckle-head, and sure enough he was sportin' a jockey shift. I had a brown paper sack that was holding a quarter pound and two thousand dollars.

"Michele, get Eddie a mug, wouldja?"

There was a frosty pitcher sitting in front of Gator and he poured me full. "Runnin' With The Devil" was on blast from the jukebox. Man, the devil sure had some good music. I handed the bag to Gator.

"I don't know what fingers go for, but maybe this will help."

Gator opened the bag and took a peek. He turned his face toward me and looked away quick, then he rolled that bag up tight. He was concentrating really hard on getting the hair tie out of his ponytail and cinching it around that bag.

"Michele, put this someplace safe and don't be snoopin' and if you do snoop don't snoop more than a gram or yer in deep trouble."

"Thanks, honey."

Michele ran the bar for the owners Patti and Jerry and she ran it really well. The Port 17 was the quintessential biker bar. Anyone was welcome but you had better understand the nuances of biker etiquette. There was a definite test. A stranger was allowed to play pool, play the jukebox, rest his elbows on the bar, but he would be watched, carefully. If he was quiet, didn't get stupid drunk, didn't ask about drugs, didn't refuse drugs if offered, and did not hit on the ladies, after a couple of hours someone would probably speak to him.

There were, at the very most, a couple of hundred serious bikers in Orange County at the time and we all knew each other so to be a stranger you had to be new to the scene or new to the area. There were six or seven true biker bars in the OC: The Port, the Chez Paris, the Road's End, the Outpost, the Silver Dollar, and out in Trabuco the Alpine Inn and Cook's Corner. Each of those joints had their own crew. On a Saturday night most everybody would go around and visit each other, smoke some weed, do a couple of lines, or get in a fight or two, but there were rarely any new faces.

The vetting process was pretty strict and at The Port the person with the final say was Michele. She was so observant. Even running pitchers up and down the bar, getting quarters for the pool table and the jukebox, and mopping up puke she never missed a thing. If she went to the jukebox, rejected whatever was playing and put on "You Never Even Called Me By My Name" by David Allen Coe the next person she put a pitcher in front of had passed the test. It could take a week or it could take a month. Until that happened any inquiries about drugs, work, women, or bike parts were met with a serious shutdown and, if it persisted, a knuckle sandwich.

Consequently we were never infiltrated. If a guy presented certain curiosities he'd get set up with one of the girls and when she found out his name and his address we'd check him out. The ladies had an entirely different method for sorting out new girls and it involved a lot of time in the ladies room with each of the girls. They found out whatever needed to be found out PDQ.

Michele was Gator's old lady and so Gator had kind of commandeered the bar's office as his own. If I needed it I could use it. He caught me slamming in there once and he got pretty ticked off but he got over it quick. Quick like it took me five minutes to get him to try it, and then he followed me around like a hungry puppy dog until I gave him the bad-girlfriend speech. He was smart and quit while he was ahead but once in a while if I asked to use the office he'd shoot me a little sign in code and we'd partake together.

Gator hadn't looked up from his beer since I gave him the bag and his jaw was tight. I knew he was feeling something deeply. He finally looked at me and I got ready to hear some really private stuff. Transparent self-disclosure was not a bar side regularity at The Port or any of those other bars I mentioned either for that matter.

"Eddie, I…Crap I can't even hear myself think, let's go in the office and I hope yer packin'."

"I gotta go to the truck. I'll meet ya in the office."

When I walked in the office he was sittin' on the desk with the contents of the bag sitting next to him.

"If I left it with her it'd be an ounce light. I can't trust her with my dope but I can trust her with my heart. Does that make any sense, Eddie?"

I just shrugged my shoulders and got out the cooker and a couple of balloons.

"I love her, man."

"Well, talking about love, that is kind of how you came to be in possession of that gak and that cash."

That raised his eyebrows.

"You were there when I made the deal with Coyote."

"Well, I was just walking in the door but I got the gist of it. She gets rescued from a piece of crap and he gets some go-fast and a permit to keep living here."

"Yeah, well, I modified the deal."

"In what way?"

Gator's eyes were dancing merrily with glee and he was leaning way forward like if he were closer he'd hear sooner.

"I was supposed to take him a quarter pound for which he was going to give me two G's, only when he started disrespecting Shine I went up in his grill with my piece and told him he was done. I gave him a week to clear out or I was gonna punch his ticket. Of course I took the dope back and kept the money. So the upshot of all that is we're gonna have to move on him soon and I'm thinking tonight."

"I don't even know what you've got in mind."

'Trust me, yer gonna love it. Just be at the Black House about eleven and bring that Desert Eagle."

I was talking and cooking at the same time and that heroin smell made my bowels watery.

"You wanna drop a little of your glass in here?"

"Yeah, sure, but wait a second. The dope should still be yours—I mean, it was yours. No, wait a second—the money is yours, the dope is Coyote's but you stole it."

"Nah, man, it's all yours, so put a little dip in this cooker and let's get busy."

"What the hell are you guys doing in here?"

Michele was standing in the door and she was wearing the same face she had on when the sawed off came out from under the bar.

"Either come in and find out or get out and wonder."

It didn't take five minutes of convincing for her and I was pretty sure there was enough to go three ways. I drew up the whole thing and squirted back two-thirds.

"Gimme yer arm, girlie. Good, now squeeze here and close your eyes."

She sat down, stood up, walked in a little circle, sat down, stood up, and walked in another little circle, and sat down again as the heroin exerted its mastery over the speed.

"Nice, Gator! You just let Eddie ruin my whole life!"

Gator didn't fall for the seduction but Michele did and the last time I saw her she was walking a whore's stroll on Katella by the happiest place on earth, Disneyland, and renting a room by the hour at the unhappiest place on earth, The Caravan Inn.

It took her about a year to fall all the way and she held it together pretty good until one summer day it was about 96 degrees and Chico asked her why she was wearing a long-sleeve shirt. Jerry fired her on the spot when she took the shirt off and she just let it all go then. She had already been supplementing her income by "dating" so she just went the rest of the way. By that time my whole world had gone to "I just don't care anymore," so when Chico tried to call me out as the source of the problem I beat him unconscious and stuffed him up under his El Camino.

"Nah, babe, just one shot won't kill ya."

"That's the problem, Gator, it ain't gonna be just one shot, for reals, I'm dead!"

I could sure relate to that! My first shot had the same effect on me. The bad girlfriend gave a kind of love some people just can't quit. You've heard of love at first sight, well this was love at first fix.

"I'm sorry, Chele."

"Go to hell, Eddie, but make sure I have yer phone number before you leave."

A couple of weeks later I took her up to Martinez's pad and he was grateful. She stayed with him for a while on her way down, but a broad like that with her nose wide open is too much for any one dude, and besides, I wasn't cut out to be a dirty-leg girl's dealer. They are like vampires. Gator barely even noticed she was slowly slipping away. Real true love, right?

Every time I created another casualty I thought of Hope and I realized I was a kind of murderer. I put a bullet in you and it took you years to die. My friend Ozone loved to fight and he was a knockout artist, not surprising at two hundred fifty pounds. But he'd leave a guy in a crumpled heap on the ground and tell the spectators,

"That was actually a mystical black magic death punch. He will appear to recover and many years from now he will die of seemingly unrelated causes but we will know the truth!"

"I gotta go back to work. This should be interesting. See me before you split, Eddie."

"I gotta go, bro, Sunshine is waiting."

I just realized he had told me he loved her. Great. I came to do somebody a favor and ended up killing his old lady. Something had to change and here I was embarking on my own love thing that started out as a good deed. Was I gonna kill Sunshine too?

I looked at Gator's still bandaged left hand and I suddenly had a flash back to the time some Chicano rock band from the I.E. came and played on a Saturday night. They did a lot of Santana songs, which was one of Gator's favorite bands. I could see him standing in front of that band with the lead guitar player's Stratocaster ripping the lead from "Black Magic Woman" flawlessly. Oh man and he was good. I had a heartache. How could there be a God? Who was that that really told me, "I love you, my child"? Who comforted Sunshine after she was abused as a child, telling her the same thing? A day late and a dollar short, it seemed to me. Why didn't He stop it? Why was the world so full of evil and cruelty? Why did it seem to fall on a select group of people who just didn't fit in to begin with?

"You can't play now."

"Huh?"

"Guitar, you can't play guitar. I'm so sorry."

"Dude, I am gonna be the best slide guitar player in the world. Besides, Django Reinhardt had only three fingers."

"Go home, Eddie."

"Yeah. See ya, bro."

I turned to leave, feeling really out of sorts and disconnected.

"Eddie..."

"Yeah, Gator?"

"I ain't got no money, the doctor laid me out. I was gonna lose my house in two weeks. Thank you, brother..."

That brought me some peace.

CHAPTER 20

So there she was sitting on the porch with flour on her face and this big mixing bowl in her lap, her tongue sticking out the corner of her mouth. I forgot all my troubles, but they'd be back soon enough. I stopped and idled in front of the house for a minute just looking at her. She had looked up briefly and smiled a smile of total contentment, and went straight back to her mixing.

I drove around to the back and I was suddenly confident that everything was gonna be good, really good. Maybe she was right, maybe God did bring us together. The statement she made about God coming to her was so much like my own experience, maybe it really could be. I walked up the back steps and got the shock of my life. Frog and Moose both had razor blades and were scraping the black paint off of the front windows. Moose looked up sheepishly, grinned, and shrugged his shoulders. Frog didn't even turn around, he just shook his head. The kitchen counter was sparkling clean and there was a huge bowl of fruit posted up on it. Something was cooking and it smelled amazing and there was a greased biscuit tray sitting on top of the oven. Sunshine came in and set what I now realized was biscuit dough down on the sparkling counter, threw me a quick hug, and ran off toward the bedroom. She was laughing.

I heard the bedroom door slam and I approached it full of curiosity. I opened the door expecting to see her standing there but she attacked me from behind and threw me down on the bed. She was straddling me, had my arms pinned up over my head, and was covering my face with little kisses.

"Eddie, Frog, and Moose are so nice! They carried everything in from the car and when I said we needed some light they started scraping the windows."

She fell down on top of me and tucked her head in under my chin. I could feel her little heart beating so fast and light on my chest.

"Thank you, Eddie, thank you!"

"No baby, thank you..."

At the same time we both said:

"Thank You, God."

Shine jumped up off me like a grasshopper off a hot lightbulb.

"Oh man, Eddie, the oven! I don't want to burn dinner!"

She ran out of the bedroom and headlong into Robin, forcing them into a kind of accidental embrace. I got a snapshot: Robin, all golden colored and full of darkness; Shine, all black hair and brown skin and full of love and light.

"Oh, Robin! I'm sorry, are you hungry? I made enough for everybody."

"Uh, sure. Why not, I could eat and it smells very good."

"It's just a roast, you know, all traditional with potatoes and carrots and lots of garlic. Oh, and homemade biscuits with butter and honey. Fifteen minutes, okay?"

"Just holler, sweetie..."

Shine boogied off to the kitchen but Robin lingered outside my door. She leaned on my doorjamb and poked her head inside, her grin bordering on hilarity, like she was holding back laughing with all she had.

"Eddie, she is very, very nice!"

"Uh-huh..."

Robin was a child of the devil and if I believed that Shine was a life raft for me from God and I the same for her then it had to be that there was going to be war. So far Robin had been all the way cool to Shine. Almost syrupy. So much so that it seemed like Shine actually liked her. How was that going to play out? If Robin wasn't going to bring on the antagonism from the start then I needed to be worried about a bigger strategy, a more catastrophic confrontation.

"Yeah, Eddie, she is nice and she's beautiful. Hard to believe that dude is going to let this go. I'd keep my eyes open. I am worried about her, though, Young Edward." She let that hang for a moment and then finished with, "I mean, let's be real. You kill everything you love, right?"

There it was, the innuendo was clear. She walked off toward the kitchen laughing maliciously to herself but it left me thinking that there might well come a time when I would have to kill her too, even though she didn't fit the criteria, for I surely had no love for Miss Stevie Nicks.

"These snakes really are very beautiful."

We were all sitting around the table, a table that hadn't had a meal served on it...well, it never had in all the time I knew it. When I came into the kitchen I went to grab a beer from the fridge and what used to be a cavernous space with maybe a quart of spoiled milk, a couple of beers, maybe a half a bottle of wine, and some snake venom was neatly filled with real food. Shine must have caught everybody with an unusual appetite because huge inroads were being made into the roast she made and biscuits with butter and honey were disappearing rapidly. Moose and Frog were grunting and grinding, Moose sporting a translucent ribbon of honey down his beard. Even Robin was eating. Shine had stood up and walked over to the glass case that held the pythons and confidently reached in and scooped out our eight-foot Burmese Python, "David Boa." By the time she got back to the table he had draped himself comfortably around her neck. He had turned to investigate who it was that had him and he was looking her right in the eye six inches from her face. She leaned in and kissed him on the nose and I was sitting there watching in wonder.

She obviously wanted to make a statement but without words. Looking at her it was easy to forget the truth about her past. She dressed like a hippie—even now she was wearing loose, faded 501s and a peasant shirt. She was barefoot and her hair was up in a bun. She had the fragrance of flowers, so looking at her it was easy to forget that she had been raised by whores surrounded by the filth of sick men and their depraved ideas of what was pleasurable. Forcing their twisted appetites on broken women, thinking that their money entitled them to express their sickest perversions on these girls who had no other options but to obey.

"Thank you, guys, so much for what you did. I had been praying for so long that I would somehow be set free. I was never alone for a minute. When he left he put me in a room that was totally secure. Sometimes he would be out in the shop and I would just stare at the phone, wishing I could call someone but I had no one to call. And besides, in his shop he has a phone with a loud ringer and a light that comes on if the house phone is off the receiver. Even if I could have gotten out I never could have gotten past the dogs."

In my mind I heard their jaws snap shut on Gator's fingers and I knew that they had no compunctions about eating human flesh.

"When I saw Eddie something happened in me and I went back inside and just started praying. 'Oh Lord, I don't know who this guy is but there is something about him, he is not like the rest of the men I have seen.' And then there's you two, Moose and Frog, you look scary but you are full of kindness."

"Oh, don't be mistaken, Sunshine, Eddie is definitely clogged up with a bunch of God junk, but these two guys not so much."

"Robin, I don't mean any disrespect, but God loves all of us."

"He doesn't love me, lady."

"Yes, He does, He even loves Coyote and all the men who paid for my body—a little girl's body, at that. It is never God's failure to love, it is always our failure to respond."

"Sunshine, I have sold my soul to the devil and it is way too late for me."

This was the first time Robin had ever come right out and said it, and I knew she said it to shock Shine, but also in her there was a little fear, a little sadness, a little regret.

"Robin, you can't make any deal with Satan that can't be undone by God! He is lying to you and if you allow him to keep lying to you then you are being robbed."

I didn't know what suffering Robin had endured that had driven her to such place of anger and hatred that she had become an enemy of God, signed up for the doomsday train. That she had bought the lie that the power of Satan was going to give her victory over the nightmares that haunted her, that it would give her what she needed to exact punishment on any perceived adversary, but she was face-to-face with someone who had endured at least as much, maybe more.

"Thank you very much for dinner, Sunshine, and just so you know, as for me you are more than welcome to be at home here."

She got up and left.

"Frog, my brother, would you help me with the dishes?"

"Why, yes Moose, it would be my absolute pleasure!"

Neither of them offered commentary on what had just transpired, but I knew that if Sunshine had endeavored to make a statement with David Boa she had rocketed past my expectations by a couple of hundred light-years.

"Who are you, lady?"

"I don't know, Eddie, I have never known but I am hoping you will help me find out."

"Hey, guys, we might as well talk about this now. Tonight at eleven thirty Gator, Timmo, and Mexican George are rolling over here. You know that old brown Pinto that sits in Timmo's driveway?"

"Yeah, what a pile!"

'Well, it runs good."

"So what about it?"

"Well, tonight Coyote is leaving town in that Pinto with whatever bags of clothes he can load in there and we're going to make sure that Gator is completely taken care of. That's gonna be our midnight mission. You guys in?"

Frog's response was immediate, always ready for any kind of mischief, particularly midnight mischief.

"I'm totally in!"

Moose was contemplative. He put down the dishtowel and stood staring, first at Shine and then me and then Shine again.

Moose was a very loyal man and he had known Coyote for a very long time.

"Okay, it's simple. Just thinking about what is happening right here, what was said during dinner. You guys belong together and Robin's right, Eddie: you can be one badass dude, but you do have a lot of God stuff in you. That's what makes you different. I can't help but think that if there is a God he's got his mitts all over this. Coyote's time is up. He's proven his worth—or I should say worthlessness? So yeah, I'll ride with ya'll."

He walked over and put a hand on each of our shoulders and said very quietly and even uncomfortably:

"God bless you, guys."

I was lying with Shine on the bed.

"What are you going to do?"

"He is a bad man and he needs to be put in check."

"Yes, but what are you going to do?"

"All I can promise is that I won't do anything that can come back on you, and I won't do anything that my conscience won't let me live with, but really my business with him is done. This is about Gator and the solidarity of a bunch of guys who are loyal to each other. Coyote came into town with the idea that he could set up shop and do what he pleased and for whatever twisted reason what he pleased was to cut three fingers off of the hand of a man who was raised here. It is Gator's County, our county. Gator lost three fingers on his guitar-fingering hand. He'll never again get to sit on the porch at sunset, strumming a tune for his girl. He'll never again get to blast out mean lead licks at a bar and blow everybody's mind.

"Also, by trade Gator is a machinist, a trade where fingers are very helpful.

"But beyond the fingers, the arrogance has to be answered for. This world that we live in, all of us, is held together by certain codes that revolve around respect. It is respect that has to be earned and when someone comes along and tries to gain respect by causing pain and thereby fear then the tribe must rally and put that one down. We have no room for him here and so he must go, but he must go with nothing. He has a bill to pay and the total of that bill is everything he's got.

"As far as you are concerned you are outside all of this earthly or worldly testosterone-fueled controversy. You are my prize and unless you want something he owes me nothing and I hold no debt over his head. What I have seen in you is the beautiful truth that because of all you have suffered you will make every day beautiful because of your grateful heart."

"Eddie, I have never seen a person love another person. I have never loved anyone and no one has ever loved me. I know we have only known each other for days, but Eddie I am in love with you."

"Well, this may come as a surprise to you, girl, but I have never been in love either. Not as a grown-up, anyway. There was a girl named Michele when I was in sixth grade and she was my best friend and we loved each other completely, but it was not a romantic kind of love. In a way it was like us in that we found each other at the end of a time of suffering and neither of us fit in anywhere except with each other and a small band of kids that rallied around the energy our relationship produced. What I'm trying to say is I love you too and I knew it the minute I saw you. I also knew that I would do anything to know your love."

I told her my story. I told her about the molestation that had destroyed any hope of trust in me as a child. I told her about the encounter I had with God in front of that cathedral in Puerto Vallarta, and I told her of the reaction of my father to the story of that molestation that had been instrumental in forging the character that allowed me to survive in a world that I chose—a world of drugs, crime, betrayal, and death.

Then I told her about Calvary Chapel and Craig and Leslie and how I ran when it got too real, too close.

We were sharing a pillow and lying facing each other, our lips barely inches apart and we kissed, our first kiss. There had never been a sweeter thing in my life. When we got back from Coyote's the day of her deliverance we had not touched in that way that people do, we had hugged and she had sat on my belly and lain with her head on my chest, but we were pure. That kiss was explosive; no, it was earthshaking. I felt that my heart was going to explode and I felt things in my body that I never knew existed.

"Do you want me to take my clothes off, Eddie?"

"More than I've ever wanted anything."

She rose up and began to pull at the tie strings of her little peasant shirt. I saw the leanness and perfection of her belly, her heartbeat pounding with the weight of this love. I reached up and held her hands, slid them back down and put them on my chest.

"Isn't that what you want, Eddie?"

"Yes, it is, and I know it is what you want too. But I don't want you to ever think it is something you owe me, as if you are my possession now and so you must give yourself to me. We should wait and see what God does, okay?"

She laid her head down on my chest, sighed, and whispered:

"I truly do love you, Eddie. Thank you..."

I fell into a sweet sleep with the sweet fragrance of her breath gently touching my face.

All of a sudden I was awake and it was loud. Like a Comanche war party whoopin' it up, getting themselves psyched for a raid. All coming from the kitchen. I needed a shot.

She said, "I'll be right back, gotta tinkle." She giggled her way out the door.

When she came back in I was getting ready to do a big speedball. She slipped her grip around my bicep and I pushed it all in. She was watching my face intently, no condemnation, no judgment, just looking—I guess to see if I was still Eddie after the demons hit my bloodstream. It was very strange, shooting the only thing I had ever loved in my arm while looking into the eyes of a woman who I now loved with all my being. It was a very clear-cut conflict. For the first time in so long I wondered, *Could I get clean, live normally, have a real life?*

Right at that moment the drugs were washing over me with the customary flood of power, but the face in front of me was calling to a part of me I never knew existed.

"Come on, Eddie, time's a-wasting!"

"I'm coming, boys!"

Mexican George was lighting a joint when I walked into the kitchen, and all the boys were there waiting and wearing looks of adrenaline-fueled expectation.

"So we'll wait down the street until the porch lights flash. Run it by us all one more time."

"Smitty gave Moose some blood packs from that movie he's working on and so Moose is going to screech up in front of the house, blasting the horn, with blood all down the front of his body. Coyote should come out and Moose will act wounded, talking about the cost of being his friend, and get Coyote to help him in the house. Once he's inside he'll throw down on Coyote, get him to put the dogs up, and then Moose will tie him up, flash the porch lights, and then we go in."

"We gonna kill him?"

Robin walked into the kitchen.

"You should because he could come back."

"He doesn't have one single ally in the world. We scare him bad enough and he'll never come back."

"Don't be so sure. A man's pride is a dangerous thing to damage, and a small man's pride all the more."

CHAPTER 21

"Can I put a couple of bullet holes in the door?"

"Yeah, as if that's gonna happen. But I do have an idea and I am willing to sacrifice the windshield, seeing as how I have an extra."

Moose walked around the side of the house and came back toting a double-thick slab of 5/8-inch plywood. He opened the door and being careful of the dash and the upholstery he snugged it up behind the windshield.

"That ought to keep a nine from going through my seat."

He walked around the front of his pride and joy and popped a cap right in front of the driver's seat. Unfortunately the plywood did not stop the bullet and now there was a nice bullet hole in the driver's headrest.

"I'll reupholster the whole car, bro."

"Yeah, you will, Dog, and I'll hold you to it."

We popped a couple more caps through a double-X Towncraft, using a piece of six-by-six this time to prevent holes in the back of the shirt and Moose slipped it on. We were trying to figure out how to best apply the blood packs when we heard Smitty's bagger blasting down the street.

"Just in time, bro, you should be the one to do this."

Smitty was a stuntman and had supplied the blood packs.

"You should have shot the blood packs, so now it's just about making the blood look right."

"How did you happen to be in the neighborhood, Smitty?"

"I'm comin' with. I wanna see Gator get his revenge…"

That's all he needed to say. There was an exchange of looks between him and Gator that required no words.

"We gotta go about six miles with no cops seeing that windshield because if they pull Gator over and see that shirt it's gonna be sketchy to explain. It's months away from Halloween. Let's have two bikes about a block in front to divert attention, the rest about a block behind. And Robin, you drive the Pinto so you can pack back behind Frog."

Fifteen minutes later we were at the Standard Station at the corner of Garden Grove and Beach. Gator pointed to a pay phone on the wall and said:

"I called him from that phone right there and now here we are. I gotta thank you guys, but if anyone is having second thoughts I got no problem if you bail."

Everyone just looked at him.

"Okay, you done with your speech-makin'? There's a party waiting!"

With that Mexican George torched the doobie that seemed to always be dangling from his lips.

"You ready, Moose?"

He was already rollin' and we all watched taillights glowing their way down the street. He started honking before he even got to the gate and the outside floodlights went on at the compound. Coyote came out cautiously, toting the gauge, but when he saw the bullet hole in the windshield he threw the gate wide open and ran out to the car. I have to admit I was a little surprised at the show of concern, but more than likely it was a concern for how this recent development affected him more than for the safety of the Moose man.

I could see Coyote gesturing wildly and looking around as he talked, but after a moment he was helping Moose out of the car. They disappeared inside the house and a few minutes later Coyote came out alone. I was thinking, *What the heck is happening?*

But Frog had it figured out.

"He's just gonna move the car into the shop."

Sure enough that's exactly what he did. It seemed like an eternity and I was getting nervous. Nervous about what was going on in the house, nervous about us all standing around the gas station, nervous about the safety of the crew, and then suddenly the porch lights winked on and off.

"Here we go!"

For the first time that night I noticed a little case on Gator's belt. It held a pair of those curved-blade gardening shears. He looked at me and saw where I was looking.

"Don't interfere, brother."

Four bikes and a beat-down old Pinto circled up in the yard and in we marched.

Coyote was zip-tied to one of the big chairs in the kitchen and his eyes were as wide as manhole covers.

I thought about trying to talk to Gator but before I could he had grabbed a dishrag and shoved it down Coyote's throat and quicker than I would have thought a one-handed man could manage, *snip, snip, snip*, severed digits dropped to the floor. Then a couple of seconds later, *snip* again.

"Interest!"

Coyote was passed-out cold.

"Oh man, wrong hand. I meant to do his clutch hand like he did mine!"

Gator started toward the other side of the chair, but Moose put a big paw on his shoulder.

"That's enough, my brother."

I really felt nothing in the way of remorse or sympathy. I thought of the way he regarded others and knew that he was reaping exactly what he had sown. I thought about the character of a man who would support the slave trade, capitalize on the weakness of captive young girls. I wondered how many Sunshines there had been. I felt really good. And then Robin was there with one of her vintage jars, holding its neck under the bleeding hand and collecting Coyote's blood. She sealed the jar and then yanked the dishtowel roughly from his mouth and placed the fingers in it, folding it neatly and putting all of it in her bag. She saw me watching.

"Eddie, someday I am going to have your soul, but in this I am on your side and you need some insurance he stays gone."

She held up the bag.

"Insurance…"

I got out the fixin's and started whipping up a dose. I thought it would be much easier to handle him with a big shot of heroin in him. He had a lot of pink slips to sign. There were four bikes and three cars that I knew of for sure, an as of yet undisclosed cache of weapons, and a safe. The property was another matter altogether and we would have to have a council to determine how to handle that, but I knew Mexican George was looking for a place, having just split up with his old lady. And I already knew he would take those dogs.

Moose went to the fridge and grabbed a quart of Miller High Life and poured it over Coyote's head; he came to with a plaintive whimper. As soon as his eyes were open Mexican George was on him.

"Where are those dogs and what are their names?"

"Why?"

"'Cause they're mine now, foolio!'"

George began to reach for the mangled hand and Coyote shrank back in horror.

"They're in the backyard and their names are Hitler, Stalin, and Mussolini."

"You have got to be kidding!"

We all looked at each other simultaneously, realizing that this man was a true sociopath and that whatever we did to him was well deserved.

"Let's kill him."

I thought about that for a minute but then something a Berdoo Hell's Angel named Bruno shared with me rang out in my memory. He said:

"Eddie, three can keep a secret if two are dead."

"We can't kill him. No offense, 'cuz we've all known each other a long time, but murder is a serious beef to answer for, especially since if we kill him this caper carries all the special circumstances to make it a capital case. As it is there is already a mayhem charge here and that carries a truckload of time in itself, but as much as I love you guys I'm not willing to trust any of you that far. Then there's Robin—we don't even know where she came from."

"Thanks so much, Eddie. And here I thought we were becoming close like a brother and sister."

"You know, Robin, I really wish that were true, because in spite of who you work for I have a love for you. I realized it the other night when Shine made that roast and I was watching you when she was talking about God. I realized that you had been lied to and deceived and that somewhere in your past there was a little girl who had no guilt and who had been wounded and I love that little girl. I can picture her and lately when I see you it is more often her I see. But I gotta tell you, it kills me that the same one who did the wounding is the one you serve today."

Suddenly it came to me that this was exactly my story as well. Oh I hadn't sold my soul to Satan but he had me in his grip nonetheless. I was recrucifying the Lord every day and I knew that there was no neutral territory here. There was no Switzerland. You didn't get to opt out as a conscientious objector.

Jesus Himself said it, "He who is not with Me is against Me, and he who does not gather with Me scatters abroad."

It was stone silent and Robin just stared at me and everyone else at her.

She looked at Coyote and did some kind of waving gesture over his head and he started screaming like a banshee. Then she looked at me and just walked out. Over her shoulder as she crossed the threshold at the front door she said:

"Still a lot of God in you, Eddie."

I gave Coyote his mercy shot and we began to ransack his castle. It took a couple of hours to put it all in order but at the end we had eight signed pink slips, eight guns, sixty-two thousand in cash, and in the safe was a copy of the lease to the property and, lo and behold, it was in Sunshine's name!

While Timmo, Mexican George, and Gator were throwing a duffel bag of stuff together for Coyote's sojourn, it seems they were talking.

Everyone agreed that the lion's share would go to Gator, but the three of them came into the kitchen together. Timmo hucked the duffel at Coyote and it knocked him over in his chair. No one bothered to set him upright and he was passed out both loaded and in shock. We had already decided that at sunrise we would send him off with his duffel and five grand, driving the Pinto and with stern instructions not to stop for anything until he had put at least two hundred miles between him and Orange County.

"Eddie, can we talk?"

"Yeah, boys! What's up?"

"So the lease is in Sunshine's name, right?"

"Yep."

"What do you think about the three of us settin' up here? George is keeping those dogs and they're home. There is plenty of room, we're all single, and with everything that he had in that shop it would be a dream come true for us."

I liked the idea but I was no longer the solo shot caller, and besides by rights this was her place.

"Hang on a minute, guys."

I grabbed the phone off the bar and dialed up the Black House. I wasn't sure she'd answer but she did.

"Hey, Little Bird."

"Eddie, is everything okay?"

"It's all good, babe. Listen, I gotta ask you something."

"What is it?"

"In the safe we found the lease agreement for this place and it's in your name."

"That's right! I totally forgot! Coyote has never even met the landlord, just me." Eddie, is he...?"

"No, but he doesn't feel that great."

"Part of me is glad but part of me is sad, because it is the evil in the world that makes people like him do what they do."

"Yeah, I know you're right, but this guy...well, I guess what I'm sayin' is that we all make choices and he chose to bring pain and now he's getting his share of all the suffering he's caused. To me it's justice."

"Of course you are right, Eddie, I know that. So what did you want to ask me?"

"Mexican George, Gator, and Timmo want to sublet this place from you."

"Will I ever have to go there?"

"Never, babe, except that Mexican George is the grill master and when they throw down a barbecue you might reconsider."

Her laughter was like the tinkling of wind chimes on a breezy spring day.

"That would be fine with me, love."

"Okay, I'll see you in a bit. You okay?"

"Yeah, Robin just came in and caught me playing with David Boa. I'm going to talk to her, Eddie. She has scars that look very familiar to me because I wear the same ones."

"Okay, see ya soon."

Hanging up the phone it dawned on me, how the heck did she get there from here? It was a few miles at least. Did she walk? Did she teleport?

CHAPTER 22

It had been over three months since the episode at what had become known now as The Ranch. George had renamed the dogs Buck, Raider, and Sarge. With his two pit bulls, Lola and Ryder, it really was a ranch. Those guys were livin' large and they didn't shoot dope so in spite of Shine at first not wanting to go there we were there quite a bit. I did my last shot that morning that we sent Coyote off. Oh, I snorted plenty of chiva, weaning myself off, but I had been completely clean from heroin and speed for five weeks. The first week and a half I laid in a bed of sweat with Shine mopping my brow with a cold cloth until the chills would come and then she would pile on the comforters. She was a schemer, that girl. Here's what I mean by that. A few times she disappeared and offered no explanation as to where she'd been, but there was always a sense of great joy when she would come back, like she had accomplished some great thing and indeed she had.

I had to get out of the house one afternoon. I was almost done kicking and in fact I had been on the weight pile a few times and had grown an appetite.

I cruised by The Port on my bike and there wasn't much happening so I took a ride out Trabuco to Cook's Corner. The beers were frosty and went down good so I had four. It was the first time I felt really good in a long time. I took the El Toro Road down to Laguna Canyon and for the first time in I don't know how long I watched the surf. Late-summer, midsize South swell was rolling across the reef at Brooks Street and I sat there and marinated in memories. How long had it been since I was in Laguna? I realized I hadn't been there since the night I took that little barmaid for a ride. The night I walked away from God. Suddenly I had to get home. I had to see Shine. I had to tell her that God had shown me His plan. We were still pure. Months had gone by with us sleeping side by side and we had waited and now I knew why. I was moving home. I was selling my bikes and finding a little house in Laguna and marrying her.

I flew home on wings and couldn't get my side-stand down fast enough and my bike just fell over on the shed floor. I left it lay. I ran into the house yelling:

"Shine! Shine! Where are you, babe?"

"I'm in the bedroom, silly man."

I threw open the door and pulled her into my arms.

"Are you ready?"

It was then I saw it. It was a seven-six Parrish Bolt. Craig's seven-six Parrish Bolt.

"How in the world did that get here?"

"Calvary Chapel."

She slipped me a card and I looked at it. It said *Craig and Leslie, 714-555-3344*. I let go of her and went around the bed and stood in front of the board that had been the beginning of a relationship that was precious but that I had thrown away. I picked it up, put it under my arm, and thought about having just been in Laguna and the plan that had formed in my mind. It was if God had touched the day. I set the board down and just sat on the end of the bed and the tears came.

Shine just held me and I wept. She stroked my hair and I wept. She kissed my forehead and I wept.

"It's okay, Eddie, it's okay..."

"Babe, I went for a ride today and I ended up in Laguna, and I sat and watched the waves at Brooks Street. And I decided I would sell my bikes and get us a little pad near the beach, and I would surf and get a construction job and marry you."

"What makes you think I'd even marry you?"

"Well, would you marry me?"

"That is not a very convincing proposal, Eddie."

I got down on one knee and asked:

"Sunshine, would you please make my life complete and be my wife?"

"I'll think about it and let you know."

"What, seriously?"

We were both grinning like little kids.

"Okay, I thought about and yes, I'll marry you."

We fell back on the bed and just held each other.

"Can we do it soon, please?"

'Why?"

"You know why."

"You should call Craig."

"How did you find him?"

"I just went to the women's study Friday mornings and every time I saw a girl that looked like she might know Leslie or be Leslie I asked."

"Wait, what do you mean every time? How long have you been doing this?"

"Well, yesterday was Friday and that was my fifth time and yesterday I found her. I would have found her sooner except they were in Mexico building houses. They really want to see you. Craig had me come by this morning and pick up this board and said there's waves at Salt Creek. Eddie, there is something else."

"What, babe?"

"I got saved."

Suddenly I was seeing life. I was seeing hope. I was seeing a house that wasn't black and I was seeing a family and a church.

"Call him, Eddie."

"Right now?"

"Yeah, right now."

We had one phone in the kitchen but its cord would reach anywhere in the house. And so before I could object she was placing the phone in my lap.

On the second ring I heard a voice I hadn't heard for a very long time and it melted me.

"Hi, Leslie, it's—"

"Pete—oh man, it's you! Praise the Lord! We pray for you every day!"

"What?"

"Yeah, bro, every day! Hey, check it out: Craig is in the shower. Let me talk to Sunshine, I'll see you tonight."

"What?"

"Put Sunshine on the phone and I'll see you tonight."

"What?"

At that point Shine gently pried the phone from my grip.

"Hi, Leslie! Uh, yeah, I think he's in shock. What time? Okay. Three twenty-seven Seventh Street." She grinned at me. "Okay, big boy, jump in the shower. We're going to dinner."

We pulled up to a little H.B. beach cottage at 7:00. There was a big white carpenter's truck in front and in the yard there were two little girls sitting on the porch steps playing with dolls. They had Craig's freckles and Leslie's long, curly hair, and they were absolutely beautiful.

The older of the two came bounding down the walkway.

"Are you Uncle Eddie?"

"I guess I am. And who are you?"

"I'm Sadie, and that's my little sister, Jenny."

Before I knew it little arms were round my waist and then the screen door opened and Leslie was bearing down on me at full speed.

"Hey-ho, there's my bro!"

And then her arms were around me too. Immediately following were Craig, Ernie, Rod, and Gary.

Ernie said:

"We all cut off our hair and became vegetarians, so we're barbecuing zucchini and leeks. Ever had a leek on the barbecue?"

"Huh?"

"Just kidding! Tri-Tip tonight!"

And with that I was enveloped by an outpouring of love that was reminiscent of the first time I met this crew of God lovers at that Bible Study in Big Canyon at the Richards' house almost four years earlier. There was still that same sense of purity and completeness, a feeling that everyone was completely and totally present and that each of them had no sense of self, that each heart was joined to create one organism. I remembered hearing this unity described in a teaching at Calvary once. And when I heard this teaching I was both desperately attracted to the concept and at the same time intimidated by the prospect of so much vulnerability. It was based on this.

"Now, therefore, you are no longer strangers and foreigners, but fellow citizens with the saints and members of the household of God, having been built on the foundation of the apostles and prophets, Jesus Christ Himself being the chief cornerstone, in whom the whole building, being fitted together, grows into a holy temple in the Lord, in whom you also are being built together for a dwelling place of God in the Spirit."

Amazingly I was recalling these verses from Ephesians 2 as my heart that had become so dry and parched was watered with the love of God's people. People who had been my people—and if their present actions were any sign in their hearts and minds, they still were. This came marching across the movie screen behind my eyes. Scrolling out like subtitles, like these verses from 1 Peter:.

"Since you have purified your souls in obeying the truth through the Spirit in sincere love of the brethren, love one another fervently with a pure heart…

"And above all things have fervent love for one another, for 'love will cover a multitude of sins.'"

Everyone was staring at me with such looks of satisfaction, as if something they had been supremely confident would happen just did happen.

Ernie was always the quoter of scripture and just then he said:

"From Matthew's gospel, chapter eighteen, verses twelve to fourteen: Jesus said, *'What do you think? If a man has a hundred sheep, and one of them goes astray, does he not leave the ninety-nine and go to the mountains to seek the one that is straying? And if he should find it, assuredly, I say to you, he rejoices more over that sheep than over the ninety-nine that did not go astray. Even so it is not the will of your Father who is in heaven that one of these little ones should perish.'"*

I looked over across the yard to see Leslie and Shine with their arms tightly around each other and both of them were weeping. I was dying to know just exactly what in the world was going on here. Or were we even in the world at all.

"C'mon, guys, let's hit the backyard and grill up some cow carcass, it's been marinating since Leslie brought Sunshine home from church yesterday. The father of the prodigal killed the fated calf when his son came home and though I didn't have a calf to kill I found some really choice Tri-Tip that will be more than suitable for this miraculous occasion."

I remembered being at church with Craig and Leslie and thinking that I would never have a girl like her, that we would never be two couples joined together in faith and watching each other's families grow. Sunshine and Leslie looked as if they had been friends forever. Everything about this home said love. Walking in the front door I was face-to-face with a beautiful wood carving that I recognized as being Craig's handiwork. It was a relief carving of a wave breaking in a little bay and beautifully done across the bottom it read:

Joshua 24:15: But as for me and my house, we will serve the Lord.

Could I ever be the man over a house that served the Lord? Could I ever be the breadwinner and spiritual provider for a family? I sensed Shine looking at me and I turned my gaze her way. She was sitting on a picnic bench that had so obviously also been made by Craig. She reached down and plucked a blade of grass from the lawn and wrapped it around her ring finger and I read her lips as she whispered:

"You and me, babe."

What was going on here?! I was sitting at a picnic table in the backyard of some people I hadn't seen in four years, whose lives were as far from mine as...well, let's just say they were diametrically opposed polar opposites. Just three months ago I had participated in the amputation of some fingers and the commandeering of a grip of plunder like some kind of biker pirate. I felt nothing—no remorse, no sense of shame or guilt. It was frontier justice, baby.

I had left God riding on a lightning bolt, swept away so suddenly by feelings of inadequacy and a hunger for the basest things about my carnal self. Carried off by the Santa Ana winds and a thirst for whiskey, speed, and heroin. I could have resisted. The book of James says, *Therefore submit to God. Resist the devil and he will flee from you. Draw near to God and He will draw near to you.* I had certainly not put up even the slightest fight. The wind was blowing and I allowed it to blow me away. Now it seemed as I was being pulled back into the fold with the same quickness in which I fled. But this time it seemed God had brought me a partner for the ride. A bigger reason to do right than just me. Someone to hold and guard, to care for. Everyone was looking at me with these big grins on their faces.

"What?"

Rod said, "Whaddaya mean 'what,' knucklehead? Man, we've been praying for you for four years. We had all just gotten back from surfing about noon yesterday and Les was getting home from Bible Study and she had Shine with her. Ernie was like, 'Whoa, who is that?' We all went inside and Les said, 'This is Eddie's girl.' It was pandemonium. I mean, we had prayed for you before we paddled out and we get back and here's Sunshine with this story. I would never believe a story like the one she told Eduardo my brother, except one look at her and I knew she could not lie."

'What exactly did she tell you?"

"Everything."

'She told you about Coy—"

"Everything."

Now Craig busted in. "So we hatched up this plan and sent her home with my Bolt and then went and got some grub and here we are. So I think we oughta pray because this is one ginormous miracle."

We all circled up and held hands.

"Dear Lord, oh my, what an amazing God you are! You have answered all of our prayers this day in a most amazing way. We truly are humbled by the things that are before us right now! The way You used Eddie to rescue Sunshine and then used her to rescue Eddie is outside the scope of our imaginations but You have done this to show Your glory and the deep love You have for both of them. Lord, we pray that You would cause Eddie and Sunshine to grab ahold of You so tightly that no plans or agents of the enemy could ever loosen their grip. Thank You so much for letting all of us be a part of and a witness to this enormous blessing."

That was Craig's prayer and as it went around the circle and each one prayed I was stricken by the depth and seamless continuity of God's plans. If I believed that God is omnipresent, all knowing, and orders the steps of men, which I did, then could it be that even the night I ran away He was knowing that this moment would take place? Was the life story of this precious young woman somehow designed in parallel with mine? But what else could I assume? It all seemed to converge at this point in time that was far too perfect to be random. Far too surreal to not be real. Sunshine began to pray:

"Oh dear Lord, I cannot adequately express the depth of my gratitude. I have no words. You have brought me to the place I have always wanted to be and so I see that all the nights I wept silently and prayed, wondering if You were there holding onto a couple of things that I believed You had said: that You loved me and You would save me and hold me. Lord, I lift Eddie up to You knowing You said the same things to Him. We have remained pure and I really don't know how but it has been the only purity in my life and it has come out of most unlikely circumstances. Now Eddie has asked me to marry him and I am so deeply sure that it is Your will. Lord, I pray that You break us away from the lives we have known and give us a life like You have given Craig and Leslie. And Lord I thank You for bringing us here to this place we so badly need to be. Lord, make me the woman You want me to be and the woman Eddie needs. Thank You, Jesus."

There were tears on every face. Rod left the circle and returned with two guitars and he and Leslie began to play. We ate and talked until the little girls' eyes were looking sandy with sleep and Leslie started making the prerequisite moves required to get two little girls fighting sleep into bed.

"I'll be back in a jiffy, this won't take long."

Craig stood up and scooped his babies up in his arms and together they went into the house. It was a picture I would always remember and a hope I deeply held that I could somehow have this life, that once again these would be my people and that their God would be my God.

"So Eddie, you wanna catch a surf in the morning? Say, Salt Creek?"

"How about Brooks Street? It was firing yesterday."

"You were down there?"

So I told the whole story about my revelations concerning a lifestyle change and everyone agreed that The Lord had been moving me to the very place we were all in at this very moment. Craig and Leslie came out the back door walking close, she with her head on his shoulder. They were laughing. It was the laughter of joy, a felicity that comes from being in a right place with God and with each other. Some Bible quote came to my mind and I had no idea how all this scripture could come so readily since I hadn't opened a Bible in nearly four years. But I recalled this, from Colossians, chapter three:

"And let the peace of God rule in your hearts, to which also you were called in one body; and be thankful. Let the word of Christ dwell in you richly in all wisdom, teaching and admonishing one another in psalms and hymns and spiritual songs, singing with grace in your hearts to the Lord. And whatever you do in word or deed, do all in the name of the Lord Jesus, giving thanks to God the Father through Him."

I was right smack-dab in the middle of this being lived out in these people.

What a beautiful thing that four years had passed and yet their solidarity held and grew stronger.

"Eddie wants to surf Brooks Street."

"We can do that for sure. What time?"

"Let's crack it."

"Sunshine, do you want to come hang out with me and the girls while the boys go surfing?"

"It would be really nice to be here. If you saw 'there' you'd really appreciate why!"

As we were walking out the front door Craig stepped in front of me and in his hands he held a Bible. I was shocked because it was my Bible.

"Been keeping this for you, bro."

We threw our arms around each other and just stood there like that. After a few moments Craig pulled Leslie and Shine in with us.

"Lord you know every need and every obstacle, every strength and every weakness of all of us, as well as those where these two are living. Please be a cover, be an ever-present help, and give victory where it is needed and blessing on these two. Thank You for bring us all together and thank You for Sunshine's cleverness. She found us, Lord, and we thank You for that beautiful miracle."

CHAPTER 23

Rosie rode slow and easy down Beach Boulevard and Shine was tight up against me with her head on my shoulder, little sighs of contentment pouring out of her with a very pleasant frequency. I had to marvel as I realized how all of her life contentment had been in very short supply. In the strobing effect of the streetlights as we passed them by I was looking at her hand resting on my thigh and I offered up a simple thank-you to God, and a single tear fell from my cheek and landed exactly in the middle of the part in her hair. She turned her face up to mine and I saw that she was crying too.

"Could any of this possibly be real, Eddie?"

I just pulled her in even tighter.

Coming in the back door of the Black House was like walking into a wall of the darkest kind of spiritual energy. Robin, Frog, and Moose were sitting at the table, weighing up some product and there were a spoon and a couple of outfits in plain view. My stomach did somersaults from a combination of both desire and revulsion. The treasure at my side gave revulsion the victory.

"When was the last time you fixed, Eddie?"

"Five weeks."

The dark queen was looking at us appraisingly and with an amusement that had the fragrance of malevolence kind of hovering like the barely discernible smell of a skunk that had been run over, but a good ways away. It didn't have the tang or sharpness of up-close skunk but it was there nonetheless just kind of a hint in the air. But I knew we were driving straight toward the scene of the roadkill and it wouldn't be long before the odor was overwhelming. We needed a plan and the plan that came immediately to mind was simply to move on. A little two-bedroom cottage in Laguna with a garage and a couple of off-street parking spots. Yeah, that would be just fine. I had the money and I had over a pound of product.

"The God in you both is growing and I'm not really digging it, Young Edward."

"We'll be doing our best to accommodate your sensitive sense of priorities, my dear sister. I feel the beach calling me; I feel the sea calling me to my roots."

Sunshine had been praying for Robin and I kept looking to see if there was any change. The only difference was that Robin seemed to really have a high regard for Shine, probably because after all she'd been through she was not only alive but mostly unsullied. No addictions, no vehement hatred brewing, and she loved on Robin like there was no tomorrow—which she reminded me that none of us was promised.

I could hear her in my mind saying, "Eddie, He wants everyone, that includes Robin."

I had an idea.

"Sunshine, come to the bedroom."

She followed me. I went into our room and straight to the safe under the bed. I removed the five quarter-pound bags and held a *sshhh* finger up to my lips. "Follow me." We walked stealthily down the hall and into the bathroom, where I began to pour eight thousand dollars' worth of speed down the toilet.

"Eddie, you are the craziest, most amazing man I have ever met, but then most of the men I have met have been drunks, junkies or whoremongers. Nonetheless, you are beautiful."

"I can't begin this journey with God and you and sell this demon dust."

We fell asleep that night with a peace that absolutely demolished the air of evil that was daily becoming more and more noticeable as God moved more and more in our hearts. Greater is He that is in me than he who is in the world.

Before sunrise we were on our way in the pickup to Craig and Leslie's. Golden Boy Donuts was on the way and I knew that John Banich, the owner, had been up blasting coke and frying donuts since about two a.m. They had the best apple fritters so we stopped and got a dozen fresh and warm.

When we got to the pad all the lights were on and I could hear the sweet song of little girls' laughter.

"They're up and they want to go so I guess it's all of us. Is that okay with you, Shine? I've got some blankets we can bundle up in until the sun gets hot."

I was stoked because Shine had never seen Laguna and I was eager to see how or even if she took to the place. I cracked open the box of fritters and I was suddenly the man of the hour. They were still quite warm and their fragrance filled the kitchen, blending with the smell of fresh coffee. I said to Shine:

"I feel totally free, my body feels whole, and I am going to eat two of those fritters, and then I'm going to surf at a reef I've known since I was just a kid. I'm going to show you my hometown and we are going to have the best day with the best people, and by the end of the day we are going to know which way we are supposed to go and how we are supposed to get there. Tomorrow we can go to church. Girl, we are going to have a life!"

Craig and Leslie were loading stuff in an ice chest. Some things never change. like the extra large jar of Skippy and the Smucker's strawberry jam I saw sitting on the counter next to two loaves of bread and two gallons of milk.

Rod, Gary, and Ernie were loading boards and beach chairs, towels and an umbrella. Jenny and Sadie were wrapped around Shine on the couch, a twisted knot of skinned knees, elbows, freckles, and impossibly long, curly, sun-kissed hair. I noticed that neither of them ever stopped squirming around in an intense competition to see who could hold possession of the most of Shine's lap.

"Can I call you Auntie Sunshine?" Sadie asked.

"I would love it if you called me Auntie!"

"Oh man! I don't have any trunks!"

I thought no one heard me, but a moment later Craig walked by and dropped a pair of scissors in my lap.

"Here ya go, biker boy!"

Ernie added, "Yeah, but please stay on the other side of the peak from us, would ya?"

"You are going to want to be my friend at Brooks Street, trust me!"

"Eddie, come in here, please."

I went in the kitchen and Leslie had set out several pairs of trunks for me to choose from.

"Thanks, sister."

Sadie and Jennie wanted to ride with us and so we packed into the cab of the '51 and headed out with us leading the caravan. The rest of the crew was in Gary's '67 Ford Econoline. I was in quite a state. My blood was pure, my mind was sharp, and my heart was a mixture of gratitude, amazement, hope, and love. Jenny was on Shine's lap and Sadie was in the middle. The bench seat was upholstered or frosted in girl legs. Two months ago the only girls' legs I saw were the dirty-legged kind, the kind that were fueled by the blood pumped from toxic and twisted hearts and ordered to move by minds bent and focused on only propelling them to the next hustle and consequently the next fix. Now there were six legs besides my ghostly white sticks that were seeing the first sunlight in years, six legs that carried innocence and beauty. Sunshine's perfect brown, slender, muscular legs and over them the skinned up, knobby-kneed and furry little girl legs, Jenny with her little toes scrunched up and trying to find traction in the dashboard to push herself even deeper into Shine's lap and Sadie with the stick shift between her toes like a thong. Sadie started to sing and soon we were all singing:

"*Father, I adore You, Lay my life before You, How I love You, Jesus, I adore You, Lay my life before You, How I love You, Spirit, I adore You. Lay my life before You, How I love You.*"

"Eddie, this place is beautiful. I feel an energy, it feels like a promise to me."

"That is the best news because this is gonna be home if at the end of the day you like it here."

"It's not going to take me all day to figure that out, buckaroo, I already know!"

"You guys gonna move here?"

"God willing that's the plan, Jenny."

"Can we do sleepovers?"

"You sure can!"

There were two parking places right in front of Laguna Surf and Sport and I whipped a totally illegal U-turn and snatched one up. I waited for the more law-abiding Gary to circle the block and pull into the spot I had been occupying with my body. I heard a familiar voice.

"Man, I thought you were dead. I mean, four years is a long time for you to miss the summer South swells. Oh, and look—you came home with yer very own crowd!"

Tex Haines stepped out of the doorway and threw a hug on me and said:

"We miss you, bro! Oh man! What the heck is with your legs? What's up, Casper?"

By this time we were all in a circle in front of the shop and so I made introductions.

"Guys, this is Tex, astounding surfer and creator of Victoria Skimboards."

"Hi, guys. Yeah, I remember you from a few times with Eddie at Salt Creek some years back." He nodded at Leslie and said, "You sat on the beach and played and sang, always inviting people to church. You made me a P, B, and J, and you got me closer to church than I've ever been. I wouldn't have remembered these guys 'cuz they cut all their hair off, but you I remember."

"This is my ex–hair farmer husband Craig, and these are our two girls, Sadie and Jenny."

Tex looked around and then his eyes locked on Shine.

"Eddie, please tell me this is your girl and that the two of you are moving back to town, and she'll be on the beach every day."

Sunshine laughed wind chimes and sparrow song. I chuckled and said:

"You, my brother, are a mind reader, because that is exactly the plan."

"You always bring good things to town, Eddie!"

The easy banter and the sense of home friendship was honey-coating the already sweet arrival of my tribe and I felt a deep soul peace, no trace of the torment of living a life that was totally outside God's purpose. I felt that He was paving the way, blazing the trail, and that here in this place with this woman I would be brought into alignment with His perfect plan for us.

In the book of Genesis, chapter one, verse twenty-six it reads: *"Then God said, 'Let Us make man in Our image, according to Our likeness.'"*

Most of my life I had been living as if I were made in the image of Lucifer, and there is no peace in his plans. If we were created in the image of God then doesn't it just make sense that the path to true peace, contentment, purpose, and passion would be in living according to the likeness after which we have been made?

How can we imagine that there is any real satisfaction to be had by living separately from His ways, His plans, His designs?

"So I know you guys didn't come down here to cut it up with me on the sidewalk, right? The surf is good, the tide is going to be favorable all day, and Eddie…Welcome home, bro, you are missed as I'm sure you will see as soon as you paddle out. I don't know about the rest of these guys, though."

We hauled all the beach gear down first—ice chest, umbrella, chairs and towels, and of course Leslie's guitar. Oh yeah, let's not forget all the sand castle–building shovels and buckets for the girls. On the way back up the stairs to get the boards Craig said:

"Man, it used to be you just brought your board to the beach, but now it's a truckload of gear!"

"Your family is so beautiful and I want one too, and I would gladly haul five truckloads of stuff if I could just lay my head down at night with my wife next to me and some kids sleeping down the hall."

"I wouldn't trade it for anything. The guys are all still single and they are always saying, 'Let's go to Costa Rica!' I'm thinking, 'Nah not me, I'm sleeping at home.' They all kind of live out their family fantasies through me and Les and the girls, which is totally cool because we have all been together for so long that we are family. Les loves them too or otherwise it would never work. We are like their compass, their true north. What about you, Eddie? You gonna stick around this time instead of running of when it gets too real?

"That girl is a gift, Eddie, straight from the Lord. She is supposed to be your compass, your true north. The thing is that God expects you to be the same thing for her, so you better get your heart right and lose the exit strategy, unpack the suitcase you have hidden at the back door of your heart. Eddie, I love you and you are one heck of a dude, but believe me I am going to say this with all love: Eddie you need to grow up, pick a direction and stick to it, and that direction needs to be straight toward God. Like an arrow, bro! Fast and true aiming right at the middle. You might not always hit it dead center but as long as you keep shooting straight you'll get your share of bull's-eyes."

The day was full of the greatest joy. As I paddled out to the second boil on the reef all I heard was, "Yeah, Eddie!" and "Welcome home, bro!" And of course the best thing I heard was, "Your wave, Eddie, go, go!"

From the water I could see Les putting on a little concert on the beach and Shine and the girls building sand castles and frolicking in the shore break. After about three hours of paddle-out take off, paddle-out take off, hunger and spaghetti arms drove me out of the water. I was full of PB&Js washed down with ice-cold Alta Dena milk and posted up on a beach chair, just surveying the beach, when Shine came up and sat next to me.

"So this is your heart place, huh?"

"Yeah, heart of hearts."

"Can I join the club?"

"Thought you already did."

"Yeah, I did."

"You wanna go up to that real estate office next to the Surf Shop and see what's up?"

"Let's go. Oh and Eddie, I like you much better as a surfer."

We walked into the real estate office on the corner of Oak Street and P.C.H. and lo and behold the agent sitting at the desk was Mark Miller, a guy I first met in third grade. The last thing that was said that day was:

"I'll have some places for you to look at tomorrow and we can have you in a place by the end of the week."

No handshakes, hugs instead. Leaving the office Shine said:

"Yeah, Eddie, this is definitely home."

The next morning I got up and put on a pot of coffee and the Allman Brothers' *Eat A Peach* album. I was blasting it and singing at the top of my lungs. Robin lunged into the kitchen with her hands over her ears and yelled:

"I am so glad you are leaving, this kind of stuff is intolerable!"

I swept her up in my arms and danced her around the room singing:

"Yer my blue sky, yer my sunny day,

Lord ya know it makes me high when you turn yer love my way."

She laughed, she actually laughed, and I said to her in a whisper with my lips brushing against her ear:

"Robin, my dear sister, Jesus loves you. He really does."

She pulled back and held my shoulders at arm's length and looked me right in the eye. She started to say something and then she started to cry. I tried to pull her back into my embrace but she broke away and ran back to her room.

In that moment I saw her, I saw the little girl, I saw the one He loved, the one Shine was trying to reach. Then I cried.

"Eddie, I'm late!" Shine said. "Button my dress and hurry up, please!"

"Whoa, girl! Where are you going?"

"I am going to Craig and Leslie's; we're going to Bible Study. I'll be back by twelve thirty and then we can go meet your friend in Laguna and look at some places."

I was buttoning up her dress and I told her about my experience with Robin.

"We have to pray for her, Eddie, and I am going to ask the women's group to pray for her, but I gotta go!"

She pecked me on the cheek and blew out the door. I heard Rosie start and then ease out down the road. I thought:

Might as well start packing up the garage and figuring out how I am going to liquidate a whole lot of gear the surfer Eddie won't need.

I was sweating up a storm in the shed when Robin stuck her head out the back door.

"Some chick named Leslie on the phone."

Something turned over in my gut and my heart kerchunked in a way it never had before.

"Hey, Les, what's up?"

"Is Shine there? We were supposed to leave here a half hour ago."

"She left here in a big hurry about forty minutes ago."

"I wonder what happened."

But suddenly I knew. I knew what happened.

"I'll call you in a little while, okay?"

I ran into the house and grabbed the keys to the pickup and blasted out the door. The keys jumped out of my hand and slipped between a tire and a barrel and it took a century to get them out. I hadn't cussed for a while but I was cussing then. I jumped in the truck and dropped the keys again. Finally I got it started and blasted down A Street to Warner, ran the red light at the intersection, and headed south on Beach. I was two blocks away from Beach and Talbert when I saw the flashing red lights and all the emergency and police vehicles. As I got closer I saw Rosie on her side and partially bent around a light pole.

"Oh Lord, no! Please God no!"

I thought that she had somehow gotten in an accident, but the truth would be far worse. I jumped out of the truck and ran to the scene. There were a couple of cops that I knew and was all right with. Sgt. Peter Jensen was one of them.

"Eddie, isn't that your Packard?"

"Yeah, yeah, Sarge, it is. What happened? Is Sunshine okay?"

"Is that your girl, Eddie?"

"Yeah, she is, we're getting maried."

"Eddie, I am so sorry."

"Sorry? What do you mean?"

"Eddie, she was killed in the accident."

I fell to my knees as all my bones turned to water. I heard an animal-like groan in the distance, but it was me.

Sergeant Jensen was on his knees beside me. "Eddie, who is the dude in the car with her?"

"What? What are you talking about? There's no dude, she was on her way to a women's Bible Study. We changed our lives! I'm clean for the first time ever! What is going on here? What is going on here?"

"Let me help you up, you need to see."

He led me over to two gurneys near the car. One was by itself unattended, a sheet covering everything, and I knew it was Shine. I ran to it and pulled the sheet back, and I took her in my arms and I just broke. A paramedic tried to interfere but I shoved him away and Sergeant Jensen told him to back off. I just held her in my arms and wept, but after a while I could hear moaning as of someone in great pain and I knew that sound, the same sound he made after his fingers were severed. Sergeant Jensen saw me looking at the pain-riddled face of Coyote.

"Do you know him?"

"I've never seen him before."

"It looks like he forced his way in the car on the driver's side at the light and she snatched the knife he had at his waist and went to town with it. Looks like he was stabbed at least eight times."

Coyote's eyes were locked on mine and they were full of fear. The fear of a small man caught in a small man's endeavor.

"Naw, Sarge, I have no idea who he is, but can I have a minute to speak with him?"

"Uh, no, I don't think so, Eddie."

I walked back to Shine's body and I bent down and kissed her lips. She always smelled like flowers and the faintest fragrance of honey and peppermint always were on her breath. I kissed her long and hard. I kissed her with all my heart, the way two young lovers kiss who have never compromised their purity but are desperately hungry. People may have thought it strange but Sergeant Jensen was a very good friend that day and he made room for our farewell kiss.

I just turned then and walked back to the five-window. I climbed in and started it up. In my bones there was a coldness. I was dying myself but I knew one thing had to happen and it was going to happen at the hospital.

"Eddie, are you sure you don't know that guy?"

"Never seen him before, Pete, but you know what? Thank you. I'm really glad you are here."

CHAPTER 24

A couple of days later a patrol car pulled up in the front yard and Sergeant Jensen emerged and came to the door.

"I just came by to tell you the coroner has cleared her body and you can make funeral arrangements."

I have to hand it to him. No cop could get this close to the inside of the Black House without his eyes meticulously scanning the entire area, but Pete just looked me in the eye.

"That guy is gonna be in the hospital for a while, but he's gonna make it."

I already knew all that. I knew exactly what room he was in, and in fact when Pete pulled up I was in the middle of creating a little get-well gift for the man.

"Okay, well, that's it. I'll see ya around."

"Thanks, Pete."

"No problem, Eddie."

I went back in the kitchen and prepared Coyote's gift: ten bags of Martinez's best chiva in a 3-cc syringe of bleach.

It was a very pretty morning as I pulled into the hospital parking lot. Pretty mornings were lost on me now. In my heart it was all raging storm and black clouds.

I was walking across the floor toward the elevator as the chime announced its arrival to the lobby. The door opened and there was Robin.

"C'mon, Eddie, we gotta scram."

She took me by the arm and walked a fast clip toward the exit. She reached into her purse and pulled out a 3-cc syringe identical to the one I had in my pocket. Deftly she wiped it off with the hem of her skirt and threw it in the trash.

"She loved me, Eddie...I could tell it was real...I had to do it. I hope you are not angry."

"No, Robin, I am not."

I looked at her profile and she was there again: the little girl, innocent and pure, full of light.

In me there was nothing but hate.

EPILOGUE

Eddie is in the fast lane headed for nothing good, and Eddie is the proverbial rope in a tug-of-war between good and evil, God and Satan, heaven and hell. It could go either way for Eddie. God is trying to work in Eddie's life but so are supernatural forces opposed to God that manifest themselves experientially in Eddie's life. Those actions by those forces give rise to traits that define Eddie: fear, anger, abandonment, pride—all things that are in direct opposition to the fruits of the Holy Spirit listed in Galatians 5:22:

"But the fruit of the Spirit is love, joy, peace, longsuffering, kindness, goodness, faithfulness, gentleness, self-control."

Although deep inside Eddie he has some of those traits as well, they have been buried in the muck and the mire of Eddie's experiences, many of which are the result of a seriously broken decision maker.

Eddie represents a demographic. A huge segment of our culture is lost and confined to prisons and institutions, some literal and some figurative. Eddie is the guy doing life in prison in Pelican Bay. Eddie is the guy who used to be a bad dude who has lost his mind from drugs and alcohol and now pushes a shopping cart around, talking to himself. Eddie is the guy who died of an overdose, so his friends threw his body in a Dumpster. Eddie is the girl caught up in a web of prostitution brought on by her addiction, which was brought on by sexual and emotional abuse as a young girl. But Eddie is also the tall, strong overcomer serving God with a clean conscience and a purified, renewed heart. This story and the ones about Eddie to follow I wrote for the men and women who have tried over and over to change. Everyone has given up on you. Family, friends, even the church have had enough of you. You will just never get it. Well, you *can* get it, because God loves you and His heart is for you.

As it says in 1 Timothy, 2:3-4:

"For this is good and acceptable in the sight of God our Savior, who desires all men to be saved and to come to the knowledge of the truth."

All means all, baby!

Keep an eye out for the continuation of the Dead Man Waking series and find out how things turn out for our Eddie.

May God bless you and keep you,

Peter Cropsey

ABOUT THE AUTHOR

I was raised in Laguna Beach, California, which in the late sixties and early seventies was the epicenter for the free-love drug culture. The streets were full of people fully in the throes of the hippie movement. By the time I was twelve I had taken LSD with Timothy Leary and was a daily user of hash and marijuana. By the time I was fourteen I had been arrested for felony drug charges and burglary. I had also overdosed on heroin. It was at that time in my life when two guys from Teen Challenge shared the gospel with me on the street and I knew I was hearing the truth. I accepted Christ as my Savior but it would be many years before I submitted to Him as my Lord. I spent the rest of my childhood, my teen years, and my early adulthood addicted to heroin and meth and in and out of jails and prisons. God had His hand on me the entire time and He was faithful even though I was not. By the time I was in my thirties I was so deeply involved in gangs and drugs that I didn't have one relationship that didn't revolve around drugs, prison, or gang activity. I had developed a reputation as a dangerous person and I did my best to cultivate that reputation at every opportunity. I was so far from God I thought that I would never find my way to a life outside of the bondage I was in. I paroled in 1989 from Corcoran Prison and somehow I found my way to a twelve-step meeting. I saw people there who had recovered from a seemingly hopeless state of mind and body.

I kept going back and it stuck. After I had about a year clean I went to church and God was waiting for me there. I realized that He was what I had wanted all of my life, but that I was so deeply in bondage to my sin that I was unable to be accountable to any relationship, let alone a relationship with God. Since I was sober I was able to be accountable and I recommitted my life to Jesus. In 1996 I began attending Calvary Chapel Laguna Beach and in 1999 I enrolled in the Calvary Chapel School of Ministry. I graduated in 2001 and went to the North Shore of Kauai to plant Calvary Chapel North Shore. I pastored there for two years and then returned to

Southern California. My dear friend Pastor Steve Rex took over for me and the church in Hawaii is flourishing under his leadership. I still get the blessing of teaching at their church when my wife and I visit the islands. In May 2006 a friend suggested that we begin a Bible Study in our home and Brave Heart was born. I pastored that church for three years and then underwent another dramatic change in my life and realized it was time to take a step back and reevaluate the direction God had for me. It was time for me to finish *Dead Man Waking*, an undertaking that began some three years previously. Through it all what I have learned is not only is Jesus Lord of all, but He is a God of repair and restoration. He is deeply interested in our lives moment to moment and there is no part of our lives that is too big or too small for His healing touch.

He doesn't say He just wants those who are nice, or smart, or pretty. He never says He is looking for people with character or integrity. No, God wants us all. In fact, He has a special interest in those of us who the world would esteem as maybe less than.

As it says in 1 Corinthians 1:26–28:

"For you see your calling, brethren, that not many wise according to the flesh, not many mighty, not many noble, are called. But God has chosen the foolish things of the world to put to shame the wise, and God has chosen the weak things of the world to put to shame the things which are mighty; and the base things of the world and the things which are despised God has chosen, and the things which are not, to bring to nothing the things that are..."

2 Peter 3:9 expresses the heart of God perfectly:

"The Lord is not willing that any should perish but that all should come to repentance."

He is so full of grace, and all He asks of us is that we make an honest evaluation of our lives from His point of view.

1 John 1:9 says:

"If we confess our sins, He is faithful and just to forgive us our sins and to cleanse us from all unrighteousness."

Man, that is all that is required to be made as pure as snow in God's eyes.

I have a dirty, dark past but what Satan had meant for evil God has intended for good.

My King has turned my rut into a groove.

God has taken a man with a reputation of darkness and made a man with a reputation of integrity.

1 Corinthians 4:1 says:

"Let a man so consider us, as servants of Christ and stewards of the mysteries of God."

It is only by His grace and His power that in my heart of hearts I desire this more than I desire any other thing from life.

Romans 3:10 says:

"As it is written: 'There is none righteous, no, not one...'"

Also in Romans 3:23 it says:

"...for all have sinned and fall short of the glory of God."

Man, oh man, this has got to be the hardest thing to swallow, the idea that by nature we are sinners and that nothing good dwells in us.

I like to point at all of the cool things I have done for others and say, "See? I am a good guy!"

And in fact if we judge ourselves by man's standards we may just be pretty good compared to, say, an armed robber or a kidnapper. But when it comes to God we are judged by His standards and unfortunately there is no sliding scale.

God is totally holy and cannot allow any sin in His presence.

Romans 6:23 tells us:

"For the wages of sin is death, but the gift of God is eternal life in Christ Jesus our Lord."

Look, here's the thing: I have tried to get around this whole Jesus deal. I have studied a myriad of religions and philosophies looking for the truth. They all just came up short.

When I learned that the Bible was an integrated message system written by the Spirit of God as He gave it to the minds and hands of men over approximately a millennium and a half; when I realized that these sixty-six books written by forty authors as they were directed by the Holy Sprit were so perfectly interwoven that science, history, and archaeology were unable to disprove the truth contained in its pages, I was amazed.

Then there is the miracle of prophecy. There were literally hundreds of prophecies about Jesus in the Old Testament that needed to be fulfilled for Him to be the Messiah, and He fulfilled each and every one to the letter. Prophecy is God's fingerprints on the Bible and provides irrefutable evidence for the truth of Christianity.

Still, I have to tell you that in spite of all of the evidence, the thing that is the true proof is the change God brings to the hearts of all who receive Him.

You can ask the believer who has only been walking with the Lord for a couple of days. He will not know all of the theological defenses for the gospel but he will tell you that he is no longer the same. He will tell you that a hunger he had suffered from all of his life has been relieved and in its place is a fullness of joy that is quite inexplicable.

Romans 5:8 says:

"But God demonstrates His own love toward us, in that while we were still sinners, Christ died for us."

That is the most wonderful thing, the idea that God's grace provides a way for us to be reconciled to Him that is in no way related to our efforts.

All we have to do is receive this wonderful gift and then walk in it.

The work has already been done on the cross.

God cleans His fish after He catches them.

Romans 10:13 tells us:

"For 'whoever calls on the name of the Lord shall be saved.'"

Come on and call on Him right now. It is no accident that you picked up this book.

If you are sick and tired of being sick and tired, then today is the day you can enter into a relationship with a true and living God who cares for you and has been calling you to Him all of your life.

Jeremiah 29:11 says this:

"For I know the thoughts that I think toward you, says the Lord, thoughts of peace and not of evil, to give you a future and a hope."

If you want to spend eternity in heaven with Jesus and if you want to have all of your sins forgiven you then please pray this prayer.

But remember, Acts 4:12 says:

"Nor is there salvation in any other, for there is no other name under heaven given among men by which we must be saved."

So if you are ready to turn it all around and enter into a relationship that is eternal and full of peace and passion, joy and truth, then please just pray this simple prayer:

Lord Jesus, I know I am a sinner. I believe that you died for my sins. I believe that you rose from the grave forever defeating sin and death. Please forgive me for my sins and enter my heart. I invite you to be my Savior and also the Lord of my life. Please give me a hunger for Your Word and the company of other believers. Please plant me in a church that is rightly dividing Your Word of truth. Thank you Lord for saving me. Amen."

Congratulations! You are now a member of the family of God.

Galatians 3:26 says:

"For you are all sons of God through faith in Christ Jesus."

Currently I am pastoring First Love Church in Costa Mesa, California. You can check it out at firstlovechurch.net or on Facebook (https://www.facebook.com/firstlovechurch). First Love is now four years old and is second only to my God and the family He has given me. My wife is my best friend and my co-laborer in ministry, my kids are a blessing, and God is winning! May He claim the victory in you as well!

Made in the USA
Columbia, SC
08 November 2021